PRAISE FOR RICHARD

"Spellbinding, Brilliant, Fantastic, Excellent, Richard McCann was utterly superb." These were some of the comments I received from my staff after hearing Richard speak at our annual conference. His ability to connect with the audience, having them laughing and crying in equal measure and inspiring them through his incredible life story was very impressive. Truly inspirational.

— Mark Jones, Managing Director, Wherry Housing Association

"I am struggling to find words to express our appreciation for the immense contribution you have made to Barnardo's by attending as guest speaker. Your personal experience and the honest and disarming way in which, with absolute frankness, you shared your own life's difficulties was both moving and compelling."

— Andrew Nebel, UK Director
of Marketing and Communications, Barnardo's

"Richard, your extremely poignant, and inspirational address received a standing ovation at my Divisional Sales Conference. Congratulations and many thanks. An all time NEW WEEKLY SALES RECORD last week affirms the motivational impact you made."

— George Munro, Vice President,
Northern UK Division, Combined Insurance

"Richard McCann has a magical gift that grabs his audience by the collar and has them perched in anticipation on every word. He literally captivates the listeners and has them sitting on the edge of their seats wondering what is coming next. Few speakers have Richard's unique ability. His stories capture and appeal to all who listen as he takes them on a journey through highs and lows, laughing and crying and a fabulous heart-warming positive finale."

— Mike Berry, Inspire Scotland, Edinburgh

iCan

PRAISE FOR RICHARD

"Your motivational and moving story helped to show staff how they can inspire learners to improve their lives and aim for an incredible future."
— Ann Yasin, Professional Development Coordinator,
Thomas Danby College, Leeds

"A truly outstanding speaker, a heartfelt story told from the heart."
— David Powell, JCI Leeds Business Events Director

"Richard, thank you for attending the Leadership Event on the 1st July 2008 as a pre-dinner speaker. I have event-managed over 150 events whilst working for the Improvement Foundation, and until hearing you speak at one of our events I had never seen a standing ovation."
— Catherine Bentley, Events Co-Ordinator, Improvement Foundation

"I required some powerful, thought provoking delivery in the conference to stimulate and motivate delegates in the afternoon period. Richard's emotive talk 'blew the audience away'. It created the backbone for what has proved to be a successful conference, inspiring not only thought but also action. Richard skilfully combined his own personal story with the message of the conference, in a highly professional and well constructed manner. Richard proved himself to be a highly skilled orator, who captivates an audience, commanding a strong emotional and mental presence."
— Head of Community and Business Engagement, HMP Hull

"Watching him connect with his audience is magical. He does this by being real, being authentic and by opening his heart to us; a true sign of strength. If you are booked to see Richard, climb aboard the rollercoaster and hang on tight. I can guarantee you will enjoy the ride!"
— Amanda Wingfield, Marketing and Events Manager, Leeds

SUNMAKERS

iCan

TWO WORDS THAT WILL CHANGE EVERYTHING

RiCHARD M^cCANN

iCan

Text ©2012 Richard McCann
'iCan Chronicles' text is copyright the respective contributors.
Published by Sunmakers, a division of Eldamar Ltd
157 Oxford Road, Cowley, Oxford, OX4 2ES, UK
www.sunmakers.co.uk

Tel +44(0)1865 779944

Version 1.0

ISBN: 978-1-908693-01-3

www.richardmccann.co.uk

DEDICATION

Stuart Howarth – one of my heroes. I'll never forget you mate.

iCan

ACKNOWLEDGEMENTS

Thanks to Richard Fenton and Andrea Waltz for taking time out of their busy schedule to spend time with me; Jamie Stewart for his support with my next phase; Damian Thompson for helping me gain some clarity; Justine Greenway, my personal assistant, for many years of support; Judy Chilcote my literary agent for her friendship and guidance over the years; and Tim Downes for his insights and coaching.

A big thank you to Geoff Ramm, Andy Lopata, Jeremy Nicholas and John Hotowka for their continual support in our mastermind group; to Paul Broadie for his fantastic camera-work; and to Anna Louise Crossley for taking some outstanding photographs, not only for my business, but of my family.

Another big thank you to my collaborators – Nick Hill for his help with the 'iCan Speak' Bootcamps; to Lee Jackson with his help supporting teenagers and for helping create Teenspeak; and to Angela Whitlock for help with the personal development day 'iCan Do'. You have all been amazing and it proves that the whole really can be greater than the sum of its parts.

For their friendship: Nicky Pattinson, Dave Thomas, Karen Asemper, Michiel Carmel, Stuart Powell, Charlie Daniels, Kimm Fearnley, Molly Harvey, Geoff and Helen Beattie, Heather for also acting like grandma to my children: They love you.

To all at the Professional Speaking Association. There are too many of you to mention, but countless of you have been influential in me becoming the speaker that I am.

A massive thank you to Ayd Instone for his creativity with this book and also for urging me to do it in the first place.

To my wife Helen for her continued love and support, and our three wonderful children Skye, Ellis and Isla, a big thank you for being such wonderful human beings.

iCan

CONTENTS

THE IMPORTANCE OF POSITIVITY

COURAGE CREATES SUCCESS

ACHIEVEMENT BEGINS WITH A GOAL

NEVER GIVE UP

iCan

ABOUT THIS BOOK

This, my third book, is very different to my previous two *Just a Boy* and *The Boy Grows Up*. They were about my life and what happened before, at the time and after mum was killed when I was five. I loved writing them and seeing them on the shelves in book stores, which for me particularly, with my background, was an incredible experience and achievement.

But it's *this* book that excites me the most. Reading about my life was – I imagine – very interesting and for many inspirational. I received many emails and letters over the years that confirmed this. I believe *this* book will inspire more readers.

Since writing my first two books I have begun to be asked to speak at conferences around the UK and beyond, and it's through these engagements and going beyond what is my story that I have had most success. My speaking engagements are more than just my story. I show how what I experienced has given me

insights that I would otherwise not have had, and more importantly for my audience and for you as you read on – how it might be relevant in your life.

That's why you are here isn't it? You want to be, do and achieve a little more in some area of your life. The book is split into four key areas and for each area there are a number of short stories, each with a lesson. There are many exercises throughout the book – it's one thing reading something, but you will achieve far more by applying what you have learned, or in many cases what you have been reminded of. I've written the book so that you can dip in and out of it as and when you find the time.

I wish you well as you read on. I would love to hear of the successes you have along the way after raising your game, unleashing even more potential and achieving more than you might have thought possible in the past.

The title of the book is not just an empowering affirmation that will serve you well throughout your life; it's the whole framework of this book. I must have chosen my name in a past life to be so lucky to have *I Can* within it. (Actually, I do believe we choose the life we have, but maybe that's for another book).

Richard McCann
Leeds, January 2012

THE IMPORTANCE OF POSITIVITY

FOCUS ON THE POSITIVE

My childhood was far from perfect. For the first five years, my sisters and I were considered 'at risk' by the social services. I imagine it was because there was lots of alcohol and violence in the home I shared with my three sisters and my parents. Dad left when I was four and Mum struggled to bring up four children on her own. If that wasn't bad enough, on 30 October 1975, a week before my sixth birthday, my mother went out for a night on the town and never returned. She was murdered by the serial killer Peter Sutcliffe (the Yorkshire Ripper) 50 yards from our home. In the early hours of that fateful day, my sister Sonia and I walked yards from Mum's body as we searched the streets and fields looking for her.

It's not the kind of start in life that you would wish on anyone. At the time I thought I would never bounce back from Mum's death and that I would never feel joy in my life again. But I did and I do and the difference between where I was as a child and where I am right now is astronomical.

iCan

For the first three months the four of us stayed in a children's home where the only thing we were told was that our mother had "gone to heaven and that we weren't going to see her again." We didn't go to her funeral and I wasn't told where Mum was buried until ten years later, which meant that I never got to say goodbye until then.

After Mum was killed we finally set up home with my father and his new girlfriend Pauline, and a new chapter in my life began. I have a vivid memory of telling myself when we set up this new home with Dad that Mum had been taken by God as a sacrifice to give us a better life and so that she would no longer have to experience the violence of her boyfriend.

Now I have no idea how that five-year-old boy was able to think in that way. What I believe now – more than 35 years later – is that we all have the ability to *focus on the positive*. There is simply nothing we can do about some of the things that go on around us; bankruptcy, redundancy, divorce, interest rates, sales being down. But we *do* have complete control of the meanings that we apply to the things that go on around us. And the fantastic thing is that it costs nothing to think positively. I don't know what your situation is right now, but times are tough – and that's something I do know a great deal about. Mum's death wasn't the only thing I had to deal with – more about that later – but one thing I truly believe is that we can never underestimate the *importance of positivity*.

I would like to introduce you to one of my true heroes, who knows only too well the importance of positivity – he lives and breathes it. He almost lost his life in a terrible motorbike accident in 1971 that saw him engulfed in flames after he collided with a San Francisco cable car.

I came across W. Mitchell in November 2006, after fellow members of the Professional Speaking Association suggested I attend their annual conference where Mitchell (as he likes to be known) was to be the closing speaker. At that time, I had been speaking for around 18 months, but I had only spoken at 15 events so I was still extremely green in the speaking world and had lots to learn. I went along and was blown away by the man.

His face was scarred and his fingers – which had been burnt away in the fire – were stumps. Even worse, he was by then in a wheelchair, because four years after his horrific accident he had another. He had learned how to fly and had been taking four friends for a flight in a small plane. The plane crashed off the end of the runway and he damaged his spine, which meant he would spend the rest of his days confined to a wheelchair. That's not quite true, we discovered, as he shared his story with humility, courage and with humour. Mitchell has learned how to get himself from his chair to his sofa and back again despite only having stumps for fingers. One of the things I recall from his presentation was this:

"Before my accidents I could do 10,000 things. Now I can do 9,000. I can either spend the rest of my life focusing on the 9,000 things I CAN do or dwell on the 1,000 things I can't do."

What a guy, what a speaker and what a life-changing day for me. Inspired by Mitchell I walked away from university four days later committed to becoming a full-time speaker like him.

THE IMPORTANCE OF POSITIVITY

iCan

W. Mitchell and Richard McCann

Focus on the things you CAN do

THE IMPORTANCE OF POSITIVITY

What about you?

What do you focus on – the things you can't do or the things you can? It's not about what you can't do – it's about what you *can* do. It's not about what's not working – it's about what is. Do some more of that!

I'd like you, right now, to write a list of 10 things that you *Can* do, that you haven't yet, that you believe could help you grow either as a person, or if it applies to you, your business. Then commit to doing them: write down a date for when you will complete them.

1. ....
2. ....
3. ....
4. ....
5. ....
6. ....
7. ....
8. ....
9. ....
10. ....

READ

It's Not What Happens To You, It's What You Do About It: taking responsibility for change,
by W Mitchell, 1997.

iCan

Back in HMP Leeds

SET YOURSELF FREE

I find it difficult to believe that it's been 15 years since I walked out of the front gate of Her Majesty's Prison Leeds after serving time on a drugs charge. At the time, I thought my life was over and that I would never achieve any form of happiness again. I had fallen into the wrong crowd – but I am not trying to blame any of them or the police informer who had entrapped me.

It was my fault and I take full responsibility for it.

I vowed never to step back in prison again. Little did I know that just over 10 years later I would spend considerable time giving talks in many prisons around the UK (mainly working with The Forgiveness Project) as part of the life of a professional speaker.

I know that most of you will never set foot inside a prison. You may struggle to comprehend just what it is like to be locked up, unable to go where you want to go, to do what you want to do and to simply be in control of your own destiny.

That may be the case for many inmates, but I have also come across countless people in all walks of life who, for some reason or another, are in their own prison. In their mind, they have created invisible bars that may as well be real, because they don't achieve the things that they have the potential to achieve. They don't do the things that deep down they would love to do; they don't experience in life what is missing from it.

Long before I spent time in prison I had walked around as though I was in a straitjacket in a cell. I had seen others succeed in life and achieve things. I had made friends with classmates who had things. Their parents had their own homes and cars, and went on regular holidays. This was all alien to me. I had thought while growing up that we were just different, we were the second-class citizens, I was from the underclass and that's just how things are. Some people are lucky and some people are unlucky and I was one of the unlucky ones. Of course things are very different for me now: and I know now how wrong I was.

Escape!

How about you? What things have happened in your life that might have shaped what you (wrongly) believe is possible for someone like you? Do you believe you are different to those who go on to achieve great things? Of course you're not. The only thing that is different is your circumstances. *Our past is not our future* – my story is testament to that.

We all have the potential to be, do and create more with our lives. Celebrate the fact that you are not in prison. Break down those imaginary bars and *escape*!

Release yourself

Imagine if you were locked up for 12 months away from your loved ones. The only way to be released right away is for you to write down what you would love to do or achieve if only things were different. What would it be?

Maybe it's writing a book, working for yourself, or singing in front of an audience. Whatever it is, write it here, now.

READ

Get Off Your Arse and Get Off Your Arse Too
by Brad Burton.
4publishing, 2009 & 2011

iCan

BE POSITIVE

> *"Accentuate the positive*
> *Eliminate the negative*
> *Latch on to the affirmative*
> *Don't mess with Mister In-Between"*
>
> – Johnny Mercer

When I was younger I was often teased with names like 'Duracell' due to my dazzling ginger hair. (The long-lasting batteries were copper in colour at the top.) I hated my ginger hair when I was a child, but I now have three wonderful ginger-haired children and I'm very proud of our hair colour.

The thing about a Duracell battery, or any other battery for that matter, is that they need both negative and positive terminals to work. As a motivational speaker I often talk about the importance of having a positive attitude when those negative things happen in our lives. How much easier life could be if we accepted that we will have our fair share of both negative and positive events.

iCan

If I look back over my life I could probably draw a graph going up and down tracking the positive and negative life events that have occurred. After every negative experience there has always been a period of recovery until finally I would be in a good place again.

I remember just after the credit crunch it was announced on the news that we were still in recession. There was the usual flurry of headlines for a couple of days, but what none of the headlines seemed to point out was that the negative growth experienced during the last quarter was less than the previous quarter. This meant that if things continued at this rate we would soon return to positive growth. If only the media had reported that we were heading back to growth (which we were) and sang and danced about it as much as they do when they report something negative! Perhaps that would have encouraged people to get out there and begin spending again and we might have returned to growth even sooner.

In almost every place you look there is a choice as to how we describe the situation or the meaning we apply to what takes place around us. I had the pleasure of speaking for a large direct selling company who were not having a particularly good year. They seemed to have lost their 'mojo'. They talked about companies on the high street that had ceased trading on the kind of news coverage I mentioned earlier. Sales were down and many were leaving the industry.

In the previous year the company's sales figures had been the best for five years. This year's figures were still pretty good, but just not as high. If only they had not broken their sales record the previous year. There were still lots of opportunities out there. The world hadn't ground to a halt, although if you listened to the wrong people you'd have thought it. I believe by the time I was through they had found their 'mojo'. There are lots of negative news stories out there, but just as many positive ones if you know where to find them.

I'm sure we all know someone who has had something bad happen to them that turned out to be the best thing that could have happened. Many of us will be heartbroken when a relationship comes to an end. I know I was in my younger years. But if those relationships had not ended, I would not have met Helen who became my wife and gave me three wonderful (and ginger) children.

For an example of how I turned what I believed was a negative into a positive enter 'Ginger Massive' into YouTube and have a little fun.

Positive and negative

On the next page, in the left hand column, write down what's negative about your current situation or possibly what's negative about your current work. And on the right I want you to write the positive things. If you ask yourself the question you will come up with the answers.

iCan

It's quite simple. You need to ensure that your focus is on the list on the right. Focusing on the list on the left will ensure that you are one of the ones who just nearly made it. One of the ones who threw the towel in as it all became too much. One of the ones for whom success was just around the corner.

THE iCAN CHRONICLES

iCAN... DO SOMETHING TO HELP

Kevin "Banana Man" Allen

Kevin's life changed forever in 2005. Like many UK citizens he was sat at home having just eaten his evening meal and was putting his feet up to enjoy a little bit of television. What Kevin didn't know, as he placed himself by his wife with his cup of tea beside him, was that during the next 40 minutes not only would he change the course of his life but the lives of many thousands of children in a place Kevin had never even heard of.

In February 2005 I saw the terrible plight of aids orphans in South Africa on a TV documentary, and I went bananas! I watched in horror as a young boy (called Sne) witnessed his father die of AIDS in front his of eyes. He had to walk miles back to his home, a filthy mud hut with no running water, gas or electricity. Distraught and starving, he soon broke down in tears. So did I. His mother had already died of AIDS and his brave young sister tried to comfort him in vain.

iCan

The programme continued, and so did the scenes of inhumanity. Over two million children had lost their parents to AIDS in South Africa, and each one of them was frightened, alone, in poverty and starving.

Kevin's iCan moment #1

I found myself asking why the world allowed this to happen – when a voice in my head said back "why do you?" I knew from that instant I would not.

Six days later I was standing in Zululand searching for the young boy, desperate to help him. The hardest part of the journey was getting over the inhibition to just get up and go – in no small part because I lived in a small terraced house and my life savings totalled little more than £1500. It took me three planes, two days' travel, and a gruelling six-hour drive across rough terrain before I arrived in Zululand. The TV documentary had mentioned a convent in a small town called Nkandla, and I had decided my best chance of finding Sne was to track down the convent first.

The journey into Zululand is an incredible story in itself. Taking a taxi from Durban to Zululand is a bit like landing in London and asking a taxi driver if he can help you find a convent in Scotland without having anything more to go on than a nun's name!

I'm not religious and don't go to church, but by some miracle I can't explain, I finally found the convent in the dead of night, and the shocked nuns agreed to give me shelter for the evening.

I explained to them that I had seen the children's awful plight on TV a few days earlier and had felt compelled to help them in any way I could. We talked for a while and it wasn't long before I realised that this small convent of ten incredible nuns, was the first, last, and only hope for the 140,000 forgotten Zulus dying of AIDS in the town.

The next day the nuns said that they would help me try and trace some of the orphans I had seen on television only a few days earlier, including Sne. We travelled into the valleys and before long we found the Lindiwe family, who I had seen on TV also. Lindiwe was a poor mother dying of AIDS, desperately trying to feed 13 children, many of whom she had taken in after their parents had died of AIDS.

When I entered Lindiwe's hut, she was lying on the floor on a mat – obviously very ill. I passed around bananas and sweets, and gave out some of the children's clothes and toys I had brought. It was very humbling to see the immense happiness this small act brought to the children's faces.

Later, we continued our search for Sne, and as we travelled, I bought hundreds of bananas and gave them to the hungry children we passed on the roadside. The local Zulus, and the nuns started calling me "Banana Man", a name that would later stick.

We visited a small school that Sne might be attending and I found each class packed full with up to 140 children – they stood toe to toe and couldn't move; they had no desks or chairs, or even paper or pens to write with!

iCan

The sisters explained many had not been fed that day, and many were AIDS orphans who would have to beg for food to survive – or worst still do "child labour work" – another term for prostitution. Yet incredibly, it would only cost a few pence to feed each of them.

Sne wasn't at the school, but after much travelling, we eventually found him on an open plain. It was an incredible experience to find him, and I was able to provide him with food, sweets, toys and clothes.

All too soon my journey was coming to an end, and knowing that Sne was now under the watchful eye of the nuns, it was time to return home. I left this land of grief, vowing I would do all I could to help these forgotten children on my return to the UK.

I arrived home with the maddening knowledge that thousands of children were left orphaned, starving, frightened and alone – yet it would only cost pennies each day to feed them via school.

Over the next three years I would take many more incredible journeys back into Zululand, feeding over 400,000 school meals of fresh fruit to hungry children and AIDS orphans there, without any fundraising or financial support whatsoever. In this time I'd sold my home and used up most of the proceeds to help the children, and then worked an additional part-time job for nearly two years simply to maintain the food-to-school projects I had set up.

By January 2007 I was feeding a thousand children a day, singlehandedly; but I was burnt out, at my wits' end, and shamefully close to giving up.

Kevin's iCan moment #2

Then, as if by magic, I began to bump into people who knew people, who knew people, and an incredible sequence of events began to unfold.

In January 2008 I formed a charity and was by now feeding well over quarter of a million school meals of fresh fruit a year to the hungry Zulu children. But the real magic of my schemes was the ripple effect they had. Not only did they feed the children, but they encouraged them to attend school where they would gain a vital education. In turn this brought them away from "child labour work" and gave them a chance of a better future. Buying the fruit from the local fruit sellers also helped boost the local economy. Better still, I was beginning to influence other charities and local government to follow my lead and copy my schemes, meaning many more thousands of children were now being fed daily through school!

I've learnt a lot over the last four years. I've learnt our smallest action can make a big difference, and I've learnt iCan do whatever I put my mind too, no matter how daunting it may seem.

www.bananaappeal.org.uk

Bananaman
Kevin Allen
Ecademy Press, 2007

iCan

DON'T STOP IN A JOB YOU HATE

I was driving down the A1 from a speaking engagement. It was late and I had not eaten. When I'm speaking I find that the adrenaline will not allow me to eat. I was relieved to see that in four miles I would find a service station. I could hear the applause in my stomach at the thought of food. Four miles later I arrived and pulled in off the slip road, parked my car and made my way inside. There was no one at the counter when I arrived so I waited for a few minutes before I began to get slightly worried.

I looked around and there wasn't a soul to be seen. Then a young lady made her way towards me from my side of the counter. As she approached me I gave her a big beaming smile. She just looked at me with a serious face. I thought something must be wrong. Finally she arrived at her side of the counter and looked at me saying nothing. I paused before I gave her my most enthusiastic 'Hello' – as if to ask her where her manners were. Uncomfortably I asked for my food and got no 'please' or 'thank you' from her. She gave me my food and told me how much it was going to cost me. I couldn't take any more of this poor customer service. I found the courage to ask her if she actually enjoyed her job.

"I just want to go home," she replied. I was astonished. I paid for my food and made my way to a table as far away as possible from this negativity. I didn't want to catch it. In the centre of the table was a small container for litter. This service station had a customer service guarantee printed on the container. If you were in any way dissatisfied with either the food or service received, you were entitled to your money back with no quibbles. It's a great marketing idea – just as long as all your staff know about it. She really did let the company down. I'm sure whoever came up with the idea for a guarantee would have been horrified at her poor customer service. I didn't demand my money back – I just ate my food and got back on the road.

The next day I was speaking in Huddersfield and on my way back I called in to the Welcome Break service station. It was aptly named as I could not have been made to feel more welcome. A young lady served me with a big beaming smile, and because I had my briefcase with me, I struggled to carry the tray of food. I couldn't believe what this young lady did. She made her way to my side of the counter and said "I'll get that for you". She took hold of my tray of food and escorted me to my seat and placed the tray on the table. I was so moved by the outstanding service I received that I almost burst into tears.

What a difference compared with what had taken place around 12 hours earlier! After my meal I took one of the cards that you often see in places like this for giving any feedback. I **VERY** had to put my feelings into words so that Jenny would receive some recognition for her efforts.

WELCOMEBREAK

All too often I hear from adults who are unhappy in their work. I was a great example of this while I worked in a kitchen in a hotel in Leeds. It wasn't the greatest job in the world, but I knew that it wasn't going to be a job for life. So while I was there I gave it the best I could.

Move out, move up

Don't end up doing a job that you hate doing, or risk leaving people feeling how I felt after my extremely poor service. I certainly won't be eating there again – unless I fall on hard times and want a free meal. If you find yourself in a place that you are not happy with or doing a job that you are unhappy with, there is always something that you can do about it. Yes, it might be difficult, you might have to take one step backwards before you see any clear signs of improvement, but that's often the price we have to pay to make a change.

Or it may be that the job in question is a temporary stop gap until you are able to pursue something else or it's giving you some work experience or even life experience. Try and make the best job out of everything that you do.

iCan

Be outstanding

What 3 things could you do in your current role or as a parent, brother, child that would demonstrate that you are being the best at what you are doing?

1 ....

2 ....

3 ....

DO MORE

I like a nice clean set of wheels on my car. I once heard that a car's wheels are like a man's shoes. They are always noticed. Like me, you have probably noticed the increase in those hand car washes in recent years.

Having children now, and an extremely busy life, I just don't have the time to wash my car, so recently I popped into my local hand car wash to get it cleaned. I have so many to choose from close to my home. I could not believe it when I got home that the alloy wheels of my car were still dirty. Of course it didn't make sense driving all the way back, so I finished them myself. Needless to say I didn't return there the next time she needed cleaning. I went to one a little further away from home. This time, before driving away, I stepped out of the car. Again I couldn't believe it – the wheels still had dirt in the corners of the spokes. Calmly I asked the man who had taken my money to pop over so that I could show him something. He wasn't interested. He said "We wash cars, not wheels." I couldn't believe his attitude and I vowed, as I drove away, that I would never return there, either.

A few weeks later it was time to get the car washed once more. I drove to one of the other car washes, which I had not yet visited. As the man, from some east European country, took my money, I asked if he would ensure my wheels were cleaned. "Sure," he replied.

iCan

"Let's see," I thought to myself. The car was washed in good time and I was shepherded to the area where someone was to dry the car with a chamois leather. I could not wait to see the results after he had finished. Imagine my surprise when the man with the chamois opened my car door. Cloth in hand he leant over me and swiftly began cleaning the inside of my windscreen where the sucker on my sat nav had left a mark. I nearly burst into tears (I didn't). I could not believe how he had spotted an opportunity to show that he really cared about what he was doing.

He didn't stop there. He then cleaned the sills of each of the four doors and as he was doing that I stepped out and inspected my wheels. Spotless! I put my hand in my pocket to see what I had. I gladly handed him the largest tip I have ever given someone washing my car. I'm not sure what language he spoke, but if he could speak English I'm sure he would have been saying that "I can earn more than the boss pays me here." Would I return to this car wash in the future? You bet.

How can you do more?

How could you do more than those around you are prepared to do? Doing a little more may make all the difference. Today, the people who come out on top will be the ones who are prepared to put in that little bit of extra effort. I often say in my motivational talks "be the best that you can be at what you do." With that kind of attitude you won't go far wrong.

iCan

What is it that you can do to demonstrate that you are prepared to do more yourself? List 5 ideas here.

1 ....

....

2 ....

....

3 ....

....

4 ....

....

5 ....

....

Doing more than others will set you apart and when you add in the compound effect over time the difference will be enormous.

Note: I would like to point out that when I suggest being the best at whatever it is you do, that does not apply to anything that might be illegal!

The Compound Effect

by Darren Hardy

Sharon's story

An email from a parent

"Not sure if you will remember (bet you get thousands of emails) but I contacted you some time ago regarding the impression you made on my daughter when you went to speak at Queensbury School in Bradford. Just thought I'd give you an update as we were eagerly awaiting her exam results at the time. The fabulous news is she passed all 12 GCSE's with 4 A*, 2A, 1B and 3Cs. I was absolutely thrilled and I think some of the 'I CAN' attitude had a hand in it and I'm proud to say 'She Did'!

Just another quick update. I received your recent email about achieving. After reading it I decided to apply for a new job from which I had previously discounted myself. I thought I maybe was not qualified enough, as it was two grades higher than my present job and a managerial position. I applied on the day after reading the email and was interviewed on Thursday and 'miraculously' I was offered the post. I know it was not really a miracle, but I think if I had not read your email I would not have applied.

So Richard, many thanks for the nudge in the right direction."

— Sharon

I wonder how many readers of this book have not applied for a job that they thought they might not be qualified to do or – to use John Hotowka's theme, who will you read about later – seized the day. I know I have not and I bet most people haven't either. I wonder, if all those people did what Sharon did and actually applied for those jobs, how many would be successful. I bet it would be more than you would care to guess. Go on – what are you waiting for?

THE iCAN CHRONICLES

iCAN...
CLIMB A
MOUNTAIN

Jules Wyman

I met Jules through my speaking work and her story is a great example of what someone can achieve when they put their minds to it.

When you're standing on a narrow path that even a mountain goat might think twice about, and very deliberately not looking down at the sheer drop below you because you have a fear of heights, the last word you want to hear from your guide is "Goodbye".

The man who had been helping me along the footpaths that twisted precariously up into the mountains of Peru simply turned his back and left me. Up until now he had been doing a good job of keeping me moving along a trekking route that I would rather have chewed my right arm off than attempt alone.

"But you can't…where…no…" I stammered in disbelief as I watched him disappear down the route I'd just nervously edged up. I instinctively clung to the rock face for dear life, my knuckles turning white, my heart thumping blood in my ears and my eyes stinging with tears. As I hung there, frozen and more alone than I'd ever felt in my life, the all too familiar voice in my head began its onslaught.

"Who did you think you were, trying to do this?"

"You're no good at anything."

"You'll fail here like you fail with everything else you do."

"You were stupid to even try this in the first place."

So how did a young woman with a fear of heights end up glued to a rock face in Peru, her nose buried in a rare species of lichen, her wraparound sunglasses filling up with tears, her heart sinking at the thought of never making it to Machu Picchu?

Ever since I was a little girl I'd always wanted to travel to Peru. Maybe watching too many episodes of Paddington Bear had engraved the destination somewhere on my subconscious, but I prefer to think some part of me knew that up there, on those treacherous paths, my life would change. Call it destiny, call it a soul calling, call it what you will. I knew I had to go.

Somehow, though, I had reached 29 without ever getting near the country. At that time my choices were controlled by the negative voices in my head. You know the ones. The "I can't" and the "What if" voices.

iCan

"I can't go travelling by myself, I might get lost or hurt."

"What if all my money got stolen?"

" I can't speak Spanish."

"What if something really bad happened to me?"

In 2001 I came across an advert for a trekking expedition to Peru in aid of Scope, the cerebral palsy charity. The trip would be a five-days 100km, hike through the Andes mountains, camping as a group and supported by trained trekkers throughout the journey. It was the perfect solution for me. I could have my Peruvian adventure, travel with other people, and raise money for a worthwhile cause in the process.

A glossy photo of Machu Picchu was accompanied by the invitation:

"Would you like to discover the lost city of the Incas?"

"Yes!" screamed my heart. "Yes, yes, yes!"

"No! Don't be ridiculous," nagged my dominant negative voices.

"You can't raise that much money."

"You're not fit enough to walk that far."

"What if you fall and hurt yourself?"

Thankfully I listened to my heart, and booked myself on the trip in spite of massive fears and doubt.

I had just come out of a turbulent relationship, and whilst my new freedom was a relief, my self-esteem was still badly scarred. It took a massive amount of courage not to back out of the trip, and for that I have my family and friends to thank. While the voices in my head told me I was a fool and destined to fail, the real voices of love around me supported and encouraged me every step of the way.

And so, in May 2002, I approached the 60 strangers waiting by the check-in desks at Heathrow. Nervous tears started to roll down my cheeks. What the hell had I been thinking? Lifting a pint glass had been the most strenuous exercise I'd done recently, and here I was, about to fly over 6,000 miles in order to hike 100km through the Andes up to altitudes of 4,500 metres above sea level.

As I went for breakfast it felt like fear was kicking holes in my stomach, and the voices began their rant again.

"What are you doing?"

"You can't do this, it's too much for you."

"Turn back now while you can and go home where it's safe."

Again, my heart spoke to me. Through my blind panic I could sense the importance of getting on that plane to follow the longing of that little girl inside of me who still dreamt of reaching Peru. And reach it I did.

Our first day in Cusco was spent battling altitude sickness as we acclimatised to the thin air at 3,360m above sea level. Members of the group dropped one by one, with even the fittest retiring to bed in pain and nausea.

iCan

My worst battle, however, was still with the voices in my head. Our group briefing had tossed a whole new bunch of fears into the mix, and on the bus journey to our starting point I was practically banging on the windows and yelling, "Let me off!" Luckily my new friends encouraged me, and I found myself crossing a rickety little bridge with my fellow trekkers at the start of our adventure. Within seconds I was breathless. My rucksack felt like it was filled with rocks, and my entire body begged for me to stop. As more and more people overtook me the voices stopped nagging in my head and I started to say out loud, "I can't do this!" I felt like a fraud, and an absolute fool. I sat silently at lunchtime, worrying that everyone else thought the same of me too.

The pace slowed after lunch and I somehow made it to the end of day one. The sun sank quickly, and we heaved our oxygen-starved bodies into our tents straight after dinner. The next day I felt a shred of confidence return. The sense of encouragement from the group was clear, and I felt boosted by a faint sense of optimism that maybe, just maybe, I could actually do this. My hopes were soon to be shattered.

After lunch Helen, our Scope leader, briefed us on the afternoon trek, advising anyone with a height issue to stay back. My stomach lurched. I had been so focused on lagging behind and struggling to breathe that I had forgotten we would, at some point, be climbing up into the mountains. Me, the girl who couldn't stand on a chair without panicking. Luck, as it would seem, was on my side. I was paired up with a Spanish doctor who would be holding my hand and guiding me through the trickiest parts of the trek.

"Excellent!" I thought. Not only did I have a personal guide but he was one well-equipped to deal with medical emergencies. And so there we were, half way across that insane mountain path with the rest of the group far out of sight, when some invisible beeper called him away. Why he left isn't important. That he left me was absolutely petrifying. After several minutes of sobbing with fear, my eyes started to burn as they drowned in the salt water trapped in my tight wraparound sunglasses.

Jules' iCan moment

As I – very tentatively – lifted my shades onto my head, I heard a voice that was so distinct from the other judgmental voices in my head, that I thought someone from Scope had come to rescue me.

"You can do this," it said quietly. "Just take one step at a time."
I slowly turned my head and saw an empty path. I was still alone.

"Just one step at a time," it repeated. "Go on Jules, you can do this. Just one step."

The penny dropped and I realised that this was me, a positive part of me that actually liked me and wanted me to succeed.

"Come on Jules, you can do it." My heart started to do a little dance. I felt a surge of courage zipping through my veins.

"You can do it!" exclaimed the new voice. "Come on Jules, you can do this."

I gritted my teeth, took a deep breath, and shuffled my left foot up a few inches. I moved my left hand and quickly clung to a new part of the rock. Next came my right foot, tentatively sliding up to join its friend, followed by my right hand.
I did it!

I felt like a whole team of cheerleaders had exploded into a jumping, whirling, whooping dance inside of me.

THE IMPORTANCE OF POSITIVITY

iCan

"One more step!" shouted the voice with delight.

I made another slow side-step up the mountain. And another, and another, until I had crossed the mountain, all by myself. All the time I had felt my heart singing as I realised what I was doing. Step by step, I was moving forward, moving away from the terrified, self-doubting girl frozen on the side of the mountain, and becoming a woman who could believe in herself and conquer any fear.

When I got to the other side, I collapsed. Not from exhaustion, but from the sheer elation that I had actually achieved something by myself, which I couldn't have done had the doctor not left me! Now, I spend my life listening to that supportive voice and whenever I face something that initially seems daunting, I think back to that path in Peru, and I tell myself:

"I can do it. Just take it one step at a time."

www.positive-belief.co.uk

DO THE RIGHT THING

EVEN IF NO-ONE'S LOOKING

"Consider the rights of others before your own feelings, and the feelings of others before your own rights."

— John Wooden

I was sitting in my car at my local car park, enjoying a few minutes on Twitter. As I sat there, I saw a small sports car race into an empty space behind me as though its driver's life depended on it. Out of my mirror I could see her jump out of the car and SMASH! Her car door went straight into the car to her right. She jumped out and ran from her car without even locking it. Gosh, I thought, something serious is going on here. But my heart went out to the owner of the car that had just been whacked. Any driver reading will know how annoying it is to return to your car to find it dented, especially when you discover how much it costs to put these dents right. (As you will read later I am certainly no angel when it comes to these matters.).

iCan

I made my way over to the two cars and sure enough, she had caused an enormous dent. I was so angry at this woman and decided I would do what I thought was the right thing. I returned to my car and took out a sheet of paper to write out an explanation of what I had seen along with the registration number so that I could leave it under the windscreen wiper of the damaged car. It felt like the right thing to do. As I was returning to place the piece of folded paper on the windscreen the frantic lady was returning back to her car. I had been caught in the act – it felt a little uncomfortable.

"Hi, you probably didn't notice, but when you got out of your car you dented this car parked beside you. I know how that feels as it happened to me recently," I said, trying to sound non-confrontational.

She just looked at me as though she was assessing the situation to find something suitable to reply with.

"Did I?"

She looked down at the car beside hers and seemed shocked at what she had done. She explained with her rather posh voice that she had wanted to get to the bank before it closed. You see, it *was* life and death after all. She then tried to rub the dent away without any success. She must have felt as though I was telling her off as she then turned to her own car and began pointing out all the small dents that she had on hers. As if that was a good enough reason for her not to have any thought for the innocent car owner! She got into her car and raced off. I couldn't believe her behaviour.

I made my way to my office. As I parked my car, I spotted a young lady I recognised sitting in the car beside me. She was smoking and flicking the ash out of her sunroof onto her windscreen. Classy. She was one of the dance teachers who taught young children how to dance in the building where I had my office. I had recently discussed with the owner the possibility of bringing my two eldest to see if they would enjoy it. When I got out of my car I noticed that the young lady had stopped smoking but there was a half- smoked cigarette on the floor beside her door, still smouldering. I was disgusted (I know I am beginning to sound like a grumpy old man) at what she had done, so I walked over to her car and asked her to wind down her window.

"Oh hi!" she said in a very enthusiastic voice, obviously recognising me from the chat about my children attending her classes with her boss.

After I had replied with my own "Hi" I asked her if she felt it was appropriate to drop a lit cigarette on the ground. Like the older lady earlier she just looked at me while she thought of her reply. I was astonished at what she came up with:

"Yes, cos it's biodegradable."

I thought this was a terrible answer and most probably wrong. I wasn't sure whether or not cigarettes were biodegradable so I didn't want to get into a debate. I told her that we seem to have different opinions on the matter. I left her surrounded by her smoke and made my way to the entrance. One thing was for sure, there was no way that any of my children were going to be taught to dance by someone possessing such opinions.

Two different incidents – both on the same day – which were examples of individuals acting as if no one was looking or that no one was going to challenge them.

I'm not suggesting that I am an angel and never step out of line. All of us do at some stage. But thinking and writing about those incidents made me think about the things that I do or sometimes don't do.

When I was younger and driving one of my first cars, I confess that when driving out of a car park I dented a car door myself. I did exactly what that lady did and although it was an accident I did not do the right thing. I thought no one had seen me so I sped off. I hadn't been driving for long and I didn't want my already expensive insurance to be affected. As I write this I am slightly ashamed – I had forgotten all about it as it's around 15 years ago, but it's funny how writing can bring back memories that we have locked away. Three days later I received a letter from the police as someone had taken my number plate as I left the car park and I had been reported. I knew what I did was wrong and it was a valuable lesson to me.

More recently, I found four lottery tickets outside my local shop. I couldn't believe it. It was around 6.30pm so the lottery was not to be drawn for around an hour. As I put them in my pocket I wondered what would happen if I had a winner. What if I had the six winning numbers: what would I do? Well it was obvious what I would do. I would find a way of giving the winning ticket to the rightful owner. I publicly announced my find just in case I gave in and decided to try to keep the winnings. My wife completely agreed with me that we would hand the winning ticket over should it win. It felt exciting to think that if it won we would hand it back. I imagine that most people would keep the winnings, but of course it would be wrong, wouldn't it? I'm sure you would have handed it back – wouldn't you?

iCan

Be your own CCTV

Would you do anything different if you knew that all your actions were seen by others? Maybe those close to you or those who look up to you, your children or possibly your parents. One day, I decided that whether people were looking or not I would do what I thought at the time was the right thing.

Let's say your every move was being watched and the best bits were going to be played at your funeral. Would that alter what you did – or didn't do – in relation to your work?

What 5 things would you *like* to see on screen?

1 ....

....

2 ....

....

3 ....

....

4 ....

....

5 ....

....

HONESTY PAYS OFF

I believe we are all capable of making mistakes and I've made more than my fair share. I used to steal chocolate bars out of the satchels of my classmates when I was at school as young as eight years old. I had a lot of negativity in my life and I felt that I deserved a bit of joy. I feel a tad guilty about that now. A few years later, and whilst in my teens, my friend and I stole a bike out of someone's shed. While in the army I broke into a shed in Germany and stole a motorbike, but I had no idea how to get it started so I left it on the roadside. What a pig I have been over the years.

It had been 22 years since the army incident and I thought I had learned my lesson. But had I?

My wife Helen had been complaining for some time that her Sony laptop wasn't running as it should and I have to be honest and say that I should have taken it in for repair sooner. Finally I took it into PC World and I asked them to return it to factory condition, which they informed me was going to cost me £49. Begrudgingly I made the payment and I was looking forward to my wife's beaming smile when we finally got it back. I received a telephone call the next day to inform me that the hard drive had gone and we needed to purchase and fit another. (So that's what that sound was!)

I returned to collect the newly repaired laptop, which they handed over packaged in that bubble wrap I still love to pop, even at 42 years of age.

"How much do I owe?" I asked.

The assistant looked at the note on her own PC and said "Nothing, you paid when you brought it in."

"Are you sure?" I asked, to which she again informed me that there was nothing to pay. Now, I knew that I hadn't paid for the hard drive and I remembered how much the man on the phone told me it was going to cost: £79. That was it. I had given her the opportunity of charging me for what I knew I hadn't paid for, so I could do no more. "I'm out of here," I thought. A victory for the common man. I wondered whether or not I should treat myself to a new shirt.

But then another voice piped up. Was it my spirit, my conscious, the lessons my father had taught me when I was younger? I don't know, but whatever it was I knew that if I walked out of that store without paying then I was no more than a common thief. I couldn't do it. What would you have done?

I decided to tell the young lady that whatever her system told her I knew I had not paid for the hard drive so she should still charge me for it. You can imagine the look on her face. The technician had not noted that I still had to pay for the hard drive and here I was being honest and insisting on paying for it. As it happens, she knocked me £10 off for my honesty.

I had a choice to make. I had made some bad choices in the past and I wasn't prepared to keep making them. The importance of positivity is not only about focusing on the positive when experiencing something that appears negative. It's also about doing what's right, not what's wrong, acting with integrity. It's about looking at what you can do, not what you can't, finding the good in people rather than looking for fault. Whatever you look for you will find it.

What 5 moments of honesty have you noticed in your life where *Doing the Right Thing* has paid off?

1..

....

2..

....

3..

....

4..

....

5..

....

iCan

COURAGE
CREATES
SUCCESS

WHAT'S THE WORST THING THAT COULD HAPPEN?

In the previous section we looked at the importance of positivity. And before we move on, I'm not suggesting that all you have to do when faced with what appears to be a negative situation is focus on the positive and everything will be OK. I know only too well that some of the things that we go through in life can be painful and it's not simply the case that thinking in a particular way will take away any pain you may be experiencing. That would be a little naive.

What I am saying is that if you can find something positive about the experience, even if it's just that you may be able to help others who go through the same thing in years to come, then in my opinion that thing, whatever it may be, is a little easier to cope with.

When you are faced with a difficult and negative situation, it can be very challenging. You can feel as though there's no way through the situation and you may need to be courageous. As a child, that's something I became accustomed to. The first time I believe I needed to dig deep was on the morning Mum never came home.

Walking down the path on the field that backed onto the house at 5.30am in the dark was one of the scariest things I had ever done and I believe it somehow changed my perception of how scary things were in the future.

It wasn't the last time that I would need to be courageous either. I should probably explain what life was like for me after Mum had been killed and we set up home with Dad and Pauline, his girlfriend, early the following year.

During the next few years, my sisters and I were subjected to various forms of abuse – thankfully non-sexual. I had no self-esteem, confidence or aspirations. Everyone else seemed to have perfect lives and I felt that I was 'damaged goods' – someone who wasn't going to amount to anything. There were some happy times, but they were often overshadowed by a fear that another horrible episode was around the corner.

Mum's killer was arrested five years later. Soon after that, things began to turn around for me. Pupils no longer came up to me to ask if it was true that Mum was the Ripper's first victim and whether or not she was a prostitute. Dad wasn't hitting me any more, as I was growing up.

I decided I would try and break out of my self-imposed shell and do something different. Aged 11, I decided to take part in the school nativity play and to my surprise I was given the part of Balthazar, one of the three kings. I had to sing one verse on my own which, believe me, took some guts. I was terrified but thinking back I somehow got a thrill out of doing it. I was sorry that Dad and Pauline hadn't thought it a good idea to come and support me, but I didn't let their absence put me off. Finding the courage to do that surprised me, and I became a slightly more confident young person.

But the best was yet to come. During 1983, when I was 13, my English teacher Mr Hill suggested that I enter the school public speaking competition. There was no way I was going to get on the stage in front of 200 students and make a fool of myself in my second-hand clothes, ginger hair and skinny body!

Then I asked myself:

"What's the worst thing that can happen?"

The worst had already happened in my life. Instead, I told myself, "I can at least have a go." I suppose this was one of the first occasions that I said *'iCan'*. I entered and was given two weeks to learn my subject. Finally, the day of the competition arrived. We were all marched into the hall. As I sat there on the front row, my heart raced and my hands were sweating profusely as I watched my impressive competitors speak from the lectern.

And then it was my turn. I felt that I was going to faint there and then as I climbed the stairs on to the stage. I walked across it and turned to the sea of around 200 pairs of eyes staring up at me. Unlike my competitors I had no notes, no flipchart, no diagrams, no posters, no assistant. It was just me – the skinny, ginger-haired no-hoper who was never going to amount to anything.

I started speaking from the front of the stage and I spoke about one of the few things I knew a little about – pigeons. My father kept pigeons and it was my job to feed them and help out with training them. I spoke unaided for five minutes. Then I walked to the right of the stage, leaned down behind the curtains and opened the small cardboard box in which I had a young pigeon I had brought with me. It was my only prop – and a masterstroke. I could handle the bird as well as any veterinary surgeon. I opened its wings and showed the audience the pattern on them. I answered a couple of questions from the teachers and I then took the bird from the stage and headed towards the glass doors that were open at the side of the hall. I let her go. She headed home and I knew she would be there in less than two minutes. It was one of my proudest moments – until the next day when it was announced in assembly that Richard McCann had won first place.

I almost burst into tears when I heard the news. Something changed in me at that moment and I realised then that I wasn't damaged goods after all and that maybe one day I would amount to something. When I think now about winning that competition, I realise that I always had the potential to win it. I wonder what else I had the potential for that I didn't discover. Winning the speaking competition is something that will remain with me until the day I leave this planet. I learned an important lesson back then that would serve me extremely well throughout my life and will do the same for you.

Drive the 'Super Highway'

Often we are faced with opportunities that can unleash our potential and most of the time we fail to step up as it feels uncomfortable. We prefer to remain in our comfort zones, on 'Easy Street'. There is a slip road that will take us to a place that I describe as The 'Super Highway' – a place of:

- unlimited opportunities
- growth
- adventure
- excitement
- fulfillment.

It is a super place indeed. I had no idea where winning that speaking competition might lead to in years to come. What I do know is that I told myself *iCan* – and I did.

Paige Clarke in Uganda:
"There's a world of opportunities out there"

THE iCAN CHRONICLES

iCAN... ACHIEVE THINGS I NEVER THOUGHT I COULD

Paige Clarke

As you can imagine, I hear from people all the time either after they have read my books or they have heard me give one of my inspirational talks, in fact it takes me all my time replying to everyone although I do get around to it eventually. A little over two years ago I had just finished delivering one of my iCan talks at a secondary school in the north east of England and afterwards a shy young girl of around 14 came up to me as I was speaking to a member of staff to say how

iCan

much she enjoyed the talk. I thanked her for her kind words and thought to myself if she keeps that up (doing something that requires courage) then she will go a long way.

The teacher then informed me that they had been trying to encourage her to put her name forward for head girl. As I had spent the last hour trying to encourage 200 students to adopt an iCan attitude and to push themselves, to do things that those around them weren't prepared to do, I told her that she could do it and that she should go for it. I wasn't convinced that she would… that was, until I received an email from her.

Hiya Richard, It's Paige Clarke. You came into my school not so long since and I talked to you about myself going for Head Girl in my school and you asked me to email you back with the result. And I got Head Girl of my school.

But I just wanted to thank you! Because I never thought that to this day I would be able to achieve what I have. You really are an inspiration and made me believe that iCan do it and I had to have an interview and also had to do a presentation before being given head girl. After your speech at my school you made my confidence grow. I would love to be able to motivate people and make people believe they can do it so I just wanted to say a massive thank you and you're such an amazing man and a new role model in my life and I hope to see you sometime in the future.

I was so amazed by what Paige had done. She had found the courage that lies, often dormant, within each of us. Ok she might have been unsuccessful, but that's what life's about. A lot of the things we attempt are unsuccessful but we really must give things a go, just as Paige had done. I wonder what else she had not put herself forward for. You can imagine my

66

delight two years later when Paige wrote to me again, except this time she really had surpassed anything that I could have imagined for her.

Hiya Richard, It's Paige Clarke ... the head girl from Redcar Community College (hoping that you remember who I am). **(how could I forget her?)**

It's been a long time since we last spoke, but after reading your books and listening to your speech, which are both very inspirational and touching! I soon realised that I was capable of a lot more than I thought. If I had the confidence and belief within myself anything was possible. So when I became head girl I guess I wanted to make a difference, to help others realise that anything is possible for them and I guess that is what I did, I hope. Just like you I found it difficult to stand up and speak in front of people... but I just kept those two words in my head and heart. My first real challenge was to stand up in front of 300 war veterans and read out a poem (using a mic); gosh I hate those things and I guess it was daunting at first, but I did and seeing the impact I had on people's hearts and feelings, just from those few words I spoke, it really, I guess, shocked me and since that day I have driven towards helping others believe just like I now do.

My time was drawing to a close at secondary school and there still was something missing, still something that I wanted to do in my heart. I wanted to allow the teachers to realise just how much they inspire not only me but the children throughout the school. So me being me I went to the head teacher's office and said I would like to make a speech, only a short one, but it's important. He agreed and my time came where me, small Paige was stood in front of all the staff in the school (may I add in the staff room: scary stuff!).

iCan

Paige's iCan moment

I stood holding a small tree and the little piece of paper I had written on with a little note saying:

"We may not be able to fly yet, but with all your support and guidance we will grow and blossom, with confidence and pride. You are the reason we succeed."

Shaken and very emotional I looked up to see the whole room in floods of tears (oops). After seeing that it made me then realise that little words can make a massive difference.

I want people to realise that life can be hard, but you can succeed. The head teacher was soon to plant my tree at the front of the school with a plaque engraved with my little quote. This day was a massive turning point in my life.

But I guess I wasn't finished yet. There was just *one* more thing I had to do and that was to speak in front of the whole school (approx 1,000). This was my biggest challenge yet, but it was one I had set my heart on achieving, not only for myself but for the students. So the day came and I had prepared my speech. I stood up and looked out at everyone, for a moment I froze and could just hear the beating of my heart, having 100,000 beats a second. *iCan* was all I kept thinking, I finally relaxed my body and composed myself. I began:

"I want you all to remember, never give up on your dreams, when you believe you will start to achieve. A journey of a thousand miles, begins with a single step and with each step you take you become closer to achieving your dreams. Be who you want to be, don't let anyone tell you that you don't fit in or your hair doesn't look nice or you aren't cool enough. Nobody is perfect, everyone makes mistakes but never let anyone tell you that you can't achieve your dreams."

This was one of the hardest speeches I have made, as this wasme this happened to me, I didn't fit in, I wasn't ever cool enough. But I had a dream and no matter what, nobody was taking that from me and I guess I just wanted the children to feel the same. To know that they're not alone and they can do anything when they put their mind to it. I went back into the school some time after I had left and to see children running up to me saying they had missed me, cuddles, smiles. The little things that really touch my heart. Now I know, after making that speech, I may have only inspired one child maybe a 100, I will never know, but now that one child, can go on and believe in themselves and that's all I wanted. I guess I can say I did it, hey? But *you* are the reason I made the change.

I'm currently at college studying a sports diploma, teaching KS2 children and working at a local gym. I was given the opportunity by the college to travel to Uganda to carry out voluntary work with young children, helping to develop the local schools in the area and coach the children, a variety of sporting activities. Recently I ran for Student Governor at the College and I'm pleased to tell you that I was successful.

I now believe that 'There is a world of possibilities out there, never let anybody tell you that you can't be exactly who you want to be, stay true to yourself no matter what. Having the ICAN attitude can take you in directions you never thought were possible and lead you into successes you only ever dreamed you could achieve'. (That is what you helped me understand and believe Richard, and I want others to fee that too!)

iCan

My dream is to save enough money to go to America in 2012 to help young children in sport. It's not easy but I will make it happen. I guess I realised that I could achieve things I have been driven ever since. I am also participating in a 42 mile walk across the moors in aid of Macmillan Cancer Support so I'm currently in training for that. I couldn't ever put into words how much of an impact you have had on my life. Thanks to you I have been able to go on and achieve things I never thought I could! You truly are amazing and a hero in my eyes!

You see what a little courage can do. This email moved me to tears to hear how Paige had progressed. I can't wait to hear from her in another two years. And the great thing about courage, like thinking positively, it costs nothing but can bring untold riches.

CLIMB THROUGH YOUR WINDOW OF OPPORTUNITY

Four years after meeting W. Mitchell, who inspired me to become a full-time speaker, I was myself on the very same stage. Funnily enough, Mitchell had asked me to get on stage when I first met him, while people were out of the room, and imagine being on the stage in years to come. At that time, the thought of being opening speaker at that conference felt like a whole world away. But four years later here I was, terrified but courageous enough to go through with it. It didn't seem too bad. We don't become confident overnight. We need to take small but courageous steps to grow, to stretch ourselves, to be, do and become more than we were.

iCan

Alvin Law and Richard McCann

The final speaker of the day was Alvin Law who spoke about his 'Laws' of life. (I like it – if only I had a cool name with a word in that I could make a theme to work with.)

Alvin's mother was one of the unfortunate mothers back in the 1960s who, after visiting the doctor while pregnant, was prescribed a drug to help with the morning sickness. That drug was called thalidomide. It went on to be known as one of the biggest medical tragedies of all time. More than 10,000 children with severe birth defects were born during the four years thalidomide was available. Alvin was one of them. His birth mother had given him up for adoption after she discovered he had no arms. Having children of my own I can imagine how distressing that would have been for any parent. Luckily for Alvin, foster parents were found within days and his journey through life began. He puts a whole lot of his success down to the attitude of his adoptive parents because they did not let the fact that he had no arms stop him from achieving. In his teenage years he learned to play the drums with his feet and even joined a band. He found the courage to get on stage and play his drums in front of a crowd of 2,000 people in a charity fundraising telephone appeal, which appeared live on local TV. The event went on to raise over a million dollars, and his journey, becoming an international speaker began.

Playing the drums is not all he can do. Archery, playing the piano, driving a car; almost nothing is beyond Alvin. Having the courage in his younger years to take up playing an instrument despite the stares meant that one thing would lead to another. After the request to play the drums in front of a crowd. Then a National Canadian TV channel asked him to make a documentary. The rest is history.

iCan

Alvin Law's story reminds me in many ways of when I decided to write my book after Sonia my sister was arrested for stabbing her boyfriend. I knew I needed to do something to help her in some way. On reflection, writing my book was never going to stop her going to prison. Maybe I was a little naïve, but the upshot was that finding the courage to write the book and bare my soul was a pivotal moment in my life. Due to the publicity I received on radio and on TV (believe me, *that* took some courage!) I was invited to speak at my first conference, which was the start of a whole new career for me.

Find your window

In life many of us have windows of opportunity, which appear from time to time. Like the opportunity to go for a promotion, to work for yourself, to give a talk. And many people peer through the window and turn away and allow someone else to try it. They then get to the end of their life and can be found asking 'Was that it?' Well yes that was it. That's what you allowed your life to be. Others don't peer through the window - they climb through it. Climbing through the window of opportunity takes courage, but it can often take you to a place that you never knew existed.

What things do you wish you had the courage to do? Write 5 things down here as if your life depended on it and put them in the order in which you would be willing to do them if you had to.

1 ....

....

2 ....

....

3 ....

....

4 ....

....

5 ....

....

I would suggest that your quality of life does depend on it. Take pride in ticking each of them off as you achieve them. Believe me most readers will not even attempt to do them. Think about where I described previously taking part in the nativity play, despite being terrified, and where it eventually led.

Think about where you might be if you were to do those things above.

iCan

THE iCAN CHRONICLES

iCAN...
SEIZE
THE DAY

John Hotowka

Often, we believe we can't do something or won't do something because of what we think others might think of us. An iCan attitude can be about taking inspired action, surprising yourself and inspiring others to change their thinking for the better.

If you met him, you wouldn't believe that my good friend John Hotowka, professional magician and speaker, ever worried about his confidence. He takes up the story:

Why was it that so many people had more confidence in my abilities than I did? I've been described as Superman and Clark Kent. As a professional magician my job often entails presenting to audiences of hundreds. When on stage I show great confidence, presence and control. When off stage I'd be quite timid, unassuming and unsure. The magic that happened on stage was not my tricks, but the person I became – with an ability to connect with an audience and entertain.

My timid Clark Kent persona was affecting my personal life and business very negatively and I realised something had to be done. My biggest fear was trying new things and going out of my comfort zone. I tried many things from reading personal development books to going on numerous courses, including neurolinguistic programming (NLP).

I was going through many changes in attitude – some obvious and others very subtle. The changes were not occurring fast enough for my liking and I needed a sign that a change was happening. This would give me the confidence to persevere.

A friend of mine encouraged me to go on a free weekend course called The Mental Game Of Life, presented by Dr Topher Morrison. It was a phenomenal self-empowerment course, full of tools for self-development and improvement.

At the end of the final day we were all given a one million pound note (fake obviously). The tag line on this note was 'What's the value of one good idea?' On the back of the note we had to write the one thing we were going to do differently from this point on. I was always very hesitant in most of the decisions I had to make so I wrote, 'Take action. Do it! SEIZE THE DAY'.

All the attendees were given a raffle ticket and during the two days raffle tickets were drawn from a champagne bucket and the prizes distributed to the lucky winners. This was a very clever ruse by Topher to give him the opportunity to sell his products. The main and final prize was a leather-bound NLP Home Study Program, including 16 CDs, 2 DVDs and bonus CD worth over £500.

iCan

When the time came to draw this prize we all sat up, ticket in hand, fingers, toes and everything we could cross were crossed. As far as I was concerned the prize was mine, I just knew it. My ticket number 582 was THE winning ticket.

Topher's hand went in the bucket and out came ticket 391. Oh sh... sh... shenanigans, never mind. He announced the number again, but nobody approached the stage to claim the prize. "If the owner of ticket 391 is not here I'll draw it again." No one stirred, and the hand went in the bucket again.

Come on 582, come on 582.

"The winner is 5... 8 ... number 58."

NOOOOOOOO!!

"Come on 58, where are you?" Again. no one stirred.

John's iCan moment
The prize was drawn five times and still no winner. Five times, I tell ya, the tension was unbearable. Topher's hand was just about to enter the bucket again and the next thing I knew I was walking along the front of the stage, up the stairs and across the stage towards Topher. The audience applauded.

"Congratulations, you've got the winning ticket."

"No I haven't, but I'm here to claim my prize," I replied.

The audience laughed and Topher looked puzzled and took a step back.

"Look, you've drawn this five times and nobody has claimed it.

You said to succeed in life no matter how many tools we have, we have to take action. Look at what I've written on the million pound note you gave us, "SEIZE THE DAY", this course is my next step in my development. I AM SEIZING THE DAY, I have come to claim my prize."

The silence was almost tangible.

Topher thought for a moment and then he said "You know what? This IS your prize."

The audience went wild.

As I took my seat I went into shock, I couldn't believe what I'd done. The gall, the cheek, the inspiration. Many people approached me. They patted me on the back, shook my hand and some said they wished they had done the same.

Sometimes you have to just ask, *what's the worst that could have happened?* He could have said "No".

The prize was not the course, but the fact is, I did seize the day and from then on, if and whenever I want to, I know that *iCan*.

COURAGE CREATES SUCCESS

iCan

WHAT'S THE BEST THING THAT COULD HAPPEN?

Despite my successful debut as a confident public speaker as a teenager, things didn't improve quite in the way that I had hoped. What followed were years of those mistakes I mentioned earlier. I left school with no qualifications, took up dead-end jobs, had problems with alcohol, got kicked out of the army, had endless failed relationships, turned to drugs and then ended up in prison. I went way off track and hit rock bottom. That was 1997 and after a failed suicide pact with my sister I decided that I could turn it around. *And turn it around I did.*

My turnaround didn't happen overnight but took years of focus, tenacity, and determination. But I knew that with the right attitude I could make a life for myself. I did an assertiveness course, had more than two years of counselling and therapy and changed my circle of friends. I was promoted in my job, won an award for my work, set up a support group and began working with young offenders. Just when it all seemed to be

iCan

coming together, my sister Sonia stabbed her boyfriend in self-defence. When she told me what had led up to her doing that I made an instant decision that was to alter the direction of my life. I wrote a book about my life. *Writing that book was one of the most terrifying things I have ever done.*

I wasn't sure if revealing in the book that I had been to prison was going to harm my future career prospects. I found myself asking the question that I asked before I got on the stage at school at 13: "What's the worst thing that can happen?" I knew I could deal with whatever happened as it would never compare to losing Mum. Just a Boy came out in 2004. Publishing the book was both terrifying and liberating in equal measure. I no longer have to worry about what people do or do not know about my past. I am now proud of the person I have become and without doubt believe that Mum would be proud of my achievements too. Incidentally, the police did not prosecute Sonia for her act of self defence, which I believe they got right.

I thought that writing the book would probably be the end of it and that I could get on with my life: I could not have been more wrong! Around the time that Just a Boy was published I became involved with a charity that supported families who had been bereaved through murder or manslaughter and I attended one of their meetings in London. One of the speakers was a psychologist who was talking about the effects of trauma on a child. When it came to questions, I stood up and nervously asked when I would be able to put my past behind me and speak to people confidently. My heart sank when he replied that I might have to accept that I was as good now as I was ever going to get.

I came away disappointed, but determined to prove him wrong. I kept repeating that "I can overcome this fear of speaking in front of people," and I didn't have to wait long. A few months later, after appearing on Radio 4 to publicise my book, I was invited to speak at a conference for those dealing with hard-to-reach families. I nervously accepted the invitation and took along Helen, my wife-to-be, for support.

I did a terrible job at the conference, but at least I had done it. I knew deep down that if I did it enough times then maybe one day I would feel comfortable with it. I recall from reading Susan Jeffers' *Feel the Fear and Do it Anyway* that one of the ways we overcome our fears is to do the thing that we were fearful of. That same year I received another invitation to speak from the Samaritans, who I volunteered for at the time. I gave that talk, speaking to around 200 people and in many ways it was a little easier – although with someone fainting in the audience towards the end it really tested me. And the final talk of the year was to a group of students.

It was suggested by a friend of mine that I might want to take a look at an organisation called The Professional Speaking Association. I found them online and took myself along to one of the local meetings. I walked into the room of around 25 speakers and I knew instantly that I was out of my depth. Or was I? It certainly felt uncomfortable, but of course we both know that doing those things that feel uncomfortable is where we have the greatest capacity for growth. And I did grow. But it didn't happen overnight. It took many years before those nerves would move out of the way and allow me to get on with what I wanted to do.

During the next three years I not only shared my story, but I encouraged more and more people to adopt their own *iCan* attitude. To step up and do those things that make each of us feel uncomfortable. The things we've always wanted to do. To create the kind of life in which we decide what we want to do with it rather than a life of regret.

iCan

It's now what I do full-time and I have become one of the busiest speakers in the UK. I could never have dreamed of being in this place as I was growing up, when I was in the children's home, when I was kicked out of the army or when I came out of prison. *But I'm really glad I am.*

Take action

I truly hope that one day you will raise your game, will dream big and most importantly tell yourself 'iCan'. Just a word of warning: You can say *iCan* until the cows come home. You then have to step up and take some action. It's time to take action. So what is it that you are going to do? Nothing? Did you hope that by simply reading this book things would improve for you?

What action are you prepared to take as a result of reading this section?

1. ....
2. ....
3. ....

READ

Feel the Fear and Do it Anyway
Susan Jeffers
Rider & Co, 1997

iCAN...

BECOME THE PERSON I WAS DESTINED TO BE!

Debra Brown

I believe each of us goes through things in our lives and to us they can often be very painful. When I speak, people often tell me that they couldn't have gone through what I did. I suggest that they could if it happened to them and that they will have been through their own hardship. I think we all do at one time or another. It's where we grow. Debra's story really is one of pain but ultimately one of growth.

"Is there anyone else?" I hesitantly asked, scared of what he was going to reply. "Yes" he replied.

It felt like someone had slapped me across my face. I was numb, thinking about what this meant, fighting hard to hold back the tears. I knew that once they flowed, it would be hard

iCan

to stop. It was 24 June 2004 and my life would never be the same again from this moment.

Bryan and I had met on a student union trip to see Status Quo in 1977. He was from Glasgow and came to college in Burnley on block release as part of his apprenticeship. I was 16 years old at the time and he was six months older; he was my first proper relationship. Our love blossomed and two years later, he surprised me with an engagement ring. We had a long distance relationship, speaking on the phone, writing letters regularly, and travelling by train to see each other when we could.

When Bryan told me he was planning to travel around Europe, I was well up for it and we loved making plans for our big adventure. After ruling out buying an old car or going on my motorbike due to the cost of fuel and unreliability of the transport, we opted for pedal power and bought touring bicycles and panniers to hold our belongings. Once the tent, sleeping bags and cooking equipment were strapped to the bikes, there wasn't room for much more than a few items of clothing. We had saved up £500 each, which wasn't much, but we intended to work en route.

We set off on our travels in 1982 – I was 21 years old and eager to see the world. We cycled through Switzerland, down the Adriatic coast of Italy, caught the ferry to Corfu, then to mainland Greece cycling from Patras to Athens where we found work running the bar in a travellers' hostel. After three months in Athens, we headed back to Italy and cycled over the Pyrenees Mountains into France and then Spain, where we split up and decided to go our separate ways. Bryan ran out of money and returned to the UK, whilst I got a tax rebate and stayed in Spain for a further three months. During this time, we wrote to each other and as soon as I returned to the UK, Bryan came to see me and our relationship was rekindled. He proposed the night we were reunited and we were married on 27 October 1984.

Our first child Christopher was born in 1988, followed 19 months later by our daughter Emily. Everything was perfect. Life was happy. We had our ups and downs like any other couple, but we were very much in love. Life is like a roller coaster and we have good times and not so good times. What I have learnt is that you appreciate the highs more as a result of experiencing the downs. Life is a wonderful playground where we learn valuable lessons, and if we don't learn the lessons, they repeat time and time again until we get the message! Illness struck Bryan in the early 1990s and he was off work for two years, which put us under financial strain. He had drifted into depression and I knew I had to do something to change his state, so I got a new credit card and bought us tickets to see Tony Robbins who was doing a three-day seminar in Birmingham. Bryan objected to going, saying he wasn't well enough, but I'd arranged for my sister to have the children, booked the hotel accommodation, and persuaded him to come with me. And what a worthwhile investment that seminar was.

It was 1993 and by day two of the seminar, Bryan was cured of his two-year illness, and the skills we learnt enabled us to communicate with each other properly and at a much deeper level, which made a huge difference in our relationship.

Debra's iCan moment #1

That seminar saved our marriage. It was empowering, and I realised for the first time in my life that I had the power to choose how I feel.

Wow! What a revelation that was. I took control of my own life from that point onwards and used the anchoring techniques on a regular basis in order to change my emotional state. This

iCan

helped not only in my personal life but had a huge impact on my business life too. I was offered new opportunities, pay rises, promotions … and in 2004 I had just been promoted to executive director of a business support agency. I was on a roll and very excited about my new job. I shared the news of my promotion with Bryan who was very dismissive and unresponsive – which confused me. We were travelling to Liverpool together the following day as Bryan was working there and I was attending a meeting in the city centre. I tried to make conversation … about my new job, about how I was thinking of trading my car in for a newer one, about the kids … getting a response was like trying to get blood out of a stone. I was bewildered. I felt uneasy. He dropped me off and we arranged to meet at the end of the day.

On the way home, Bryan was very quiet and distant.

"What's wrong, Bryan? Is it your job that's troubling you?" I implored. His job had not been going well for some time.

"Course it's my job" he snapped, but my gut told me it was deeper than that.

"What else is bothering you?" I asked.

"Now's not the time or the place to talk about it." he replied.

"We have an hour's journey home so now is a perfect opportunity – we have no interruptions, no kids, so let's talk," I said gently.

"Everything's the matter! We haven't been getting on for the last six months," he replied.

That was news to me! I had no idea we hadn't been getting along. As far as I was concerned, he'd gone into his cave and when that happened, I gave him space. I was shocked, then I started to get a sick feeling in my stomach and intuitively knew he had someone else.

"Is there anyone else?" I hesitantly asked, scared of what he was going to reply.

"Yes" he replied.

"Is it Lisa?" I enquired

"Yes" he replied softly, "I didn't mean for it to happen, she was having difficulties in her relationship, I have been supporting her for a few months and we fell for each other. I didn't want to tell you till after our holiday."

That slap across the face on 24 June 2004 was a wake-up call for me. We continued the journey in silence, me fighting back the tears, and as soon as we arrived home, I spent the rest of the evening in my bedroom sobbing uncontrollably; I hurt so much. I had never dreamt that the man I had loved for 27 years would ever dump me. The feeling of rejection was overwhelming. I knew I needed to get the emotion out and not bottle it up and cried myself to sleep that night, keeping out of sight of the children who were now 14 and 16 years old.

I went to work as usual the next day, not showing how badly I was hurting inside. I tried to rationalise the situation. Did I want to fight for my marriage? Over the past years, we had lived separate lives. He was a home bird who liked to stay in, and I was the party animal who wanted to socialise with people and have fun. I was involved in a lot of voluntary work in the community, and also as a civilian instructor in the Air Training Corps, which met my needs for contribution, fun, adventure and personal growth. This had led to challenges in our relationship as Bryan felt that I wasn't spending any time with him. But I didn't want to spend every night in front of the TV – I wanted to experience life.

So I had two choices. I could be a "victim" like so many women are when they have been dumped, or I could take personal responsibility. But how could I take personal

iCan

responsibility when I was hurting so badly? I reflected on the tools I had learnt at the Tony Robbins seminar 11 years earlier.

"I know, I need to give this an empowering meaning," I thought, but what could that be?

Debra's iCan moment #2

Then it came to me and I said it out loud to myself, a huge grin appearing on my face as I declared "Bryan and Lisa have done me a huge favour, I can now become the person I was destined to be!"

Wow, that did it for me ... there was no stopping me now. I had a decision to make. Our two-week holiday to Tenerife was booked, departing a week later. Bryan had kept referring to pushing the boat out for "our last family holiday." When I had enquired what he meant, he said that the kids were getting older and wouldn't want to be going away with mum and dad for much longer and he wanted to make the most of this holiday. Now I understood what he had really meant.

I returned from work quite chirpy, made tea and sat down to watch TV with Bryan in the evening. We shared a bottle of wine and talked about the holiday. Lisa didn't want him to go, but we both wanted to go. We decided not to tell the children about us splitting up until the day before we returned home so that it didn't spoil their holiday.

We flew off to Tenerife on July 2 to stay at our timeshare apartment. As far as the kids were concerned, everything was normal. We didn't see much of them during the day – they preferred to do their own thing, which meant Bryan and I spent the majority of the first week together. I wanted the holiday to be a celebration of our life together rather than feeling bitter and miserable. We reminisced about our college days, the time we spent travelling, family parties ... he had a far better memory and I was grateful for the reminders. I went through a roller coaster of emotions that first week. One day we were like best friends walking around hand in hand laughing and joking, another day I could barely look at or speak to him because I felt so hurt, so alone, unloved, rejected. For the first time in my life, I had lost my appetite. I felt sick the moment I tried to eat. For a comfort eater, this was a new experience for me, and by day 6 of our holiday I had made a decision.

"Bryan, we need to tell the kids today ... I feel like I'm living a lie, I can't do this anymore."

So that afternoon, we called a family meeting on the balcony with Christopher and Emily.

"We have something to tell you," Bryan began. "Your Mum and I have decided to split up when we get back home."
Christopher looked straight at his dad and asked "Have you got someone else?"

"Yes" replied Bryan.

Then Chris asked me "And have you got someone else Mum?"
"No," I croaked, fighting back the tears.

This was one of the hardest things I had ever had to do in my life. You hear about families splitting up but don't think it will ever happen to you.

Chris and Emily were both upset and went off to spend some time alone. I felt a huge release – the thing I had dreaded most, telling the children, was now done. I could now accept what was happening and get on with my life. And I started that night by going out with the kids by myself and giving them the opportunity to ask me questions. Telling them in the middle of the holiday was a good thing in my opinion because it gave them a period of adjustment before returning home.

It was difficult for me during the holiday as Bryan was maintaining telephone contact with Lisa and the pinging of texts coming through was a constant reminder, but I reminded myself that he was setting me free, and the feeling of becoming who I was destined to be filled me with hope, and an excited anticipation about what was in store for me.

Three months after returning from our holiday, I took Chris and Emily to Tony Robbins' four-day Unleash the Power Within seminar in London, fulfilling a promise I'd made to myself when I saw him the very first time.

"This is the best investment I can ever give my kids" I'd thought at the time, "better than anything they'll ever learn at school." While at the seminar, I signed up to do Tony's Mastery University programme. This was one of the most empowering realisations for me ... I could make my own decision, I didn't need to consult anyone; I didn't have the money, but I could get it! Wow, I felt amazing. But not as amazing as when I arrived in Palm Springs two months later to do Date With Destiny; a life-changing six-day seminar. It was now December 2004. I'd got a bank loan and there I was staying in a five star resort in the USA, a place I'd always wanted to visit but Bryan hadn't.

Debra's iCan moment #3

I cannot put into words the profound impact that seminar had on me. I had so many insights ... I knew why my marriage had broken down, Bryan and I weren't meeting each other's needs – we didn't even know what each other's needs were!

I learnt about masculine and feminine energy and realised that for most of my marriage, I'd been in my masculine energy ... as a woman in business I had brought this side out and where was my feminine side? Very well hidden I can assure you! I learnt about values and what rules we attach to our values. I learnt so much about myself, and human behaviour.

I completely understood why Bryan had left me and took full responsibility for my part in that. I wasn't meeting his needs, nor he mine. I now had awareness and by the end of that amazing date with my destiny, I took complete responsibility for the rest of my life.

My life has completely changed since then. I lost three stone in weight, I qualified as a life coach, NLP and Time Line Therapy Practitioner, I left the security of my salaried job and set up my own business, Global Hugs Ltd. I have travelled the world attending seminars with world leaders, I have set up a personal and spiritual development organisation to bring world-class speakers to the North West of England, and I continue to contribute on a voluntary basis to local, regional and global projects to help make a difference in the world.

Debra's iCan moment #4

But most of all, I have discovered an amazing world that I was previously unaware of. I now have an amazing relationship with myself and the ability to offer unconditional love to every human being on the planet.

Bryan leaving me was the catalyst I needed to discover who and what I really am. And for that I am eternally grateful to him. I decided to file for divorce, and made the decision that I wanted it to be amicable and to always be his friend. I welcomed Lisa into my home and to family parties. (Why would I not? She had done me a favour – she had helped to set me free!) And that is exactly what happened. Because we create our own reality by the thoughts that we have and the decisions we make. We are not victims. We control our own destiny – whether we are aware of it or not.

Today, Bryan is in another relationship with a wonderful person who I love dearly. And I am with a wonderful man. We socialise regularly and have a great relationship. There is life after divorce. It doesn't need to be acrimonious ... you can create the outcome you want. You can choose how you feel. Your life is in your hands. We have some beautiful lessons to learn in life and our soul mates are those who help us to learn the lessons. Our soul mates can be those who hurt us the most, or who push our buttons ... look out for the messages they are giving us, and look into the mirror because all the answers lie within.

Debra celebrated her 50th birthday in February 2011 and she made some life-changing decisions: She sold her house, gave away her furniture and most of her possessions. She let go of her old married name of Brown and is now called Debra Sofia Magdalene. She embarked on a journey of further discovery, touring Europe by car for 2 months before setting off on a backpacking trip around the world. You can connect with her on Facebook. www.globalhugs.com

I love this story. Especially the note from Debra when she describes what she has discovered the most. "But most of all, I have discovered an amazing world that I was previously unaware of." I wonder how many amazing worlds are there for the taking for each of us. If only we could find the courage to climb through those windows of opportunity that appear in our lives from time to time.

LET IT POUR

One of my dreams as a young adult was to have children one day. Thankfully that dream became a reality and I absolutely love being a father. I'm learning so much by watching them grow.

One morning, I found myself learning something new again. Ellis my son had just turned three. We have tried to teach all of our children to be independent and to do things for themselves. That includes pouring his own milk into his cereal.

"I'm doing it; I'm doing it, Daddy." The look on his face was priceless. As the milk began to flow it eventually turned into what looked like Niagara Falls. "Ellis!" I shrieked in an attempt to startle him and to get him to stop pouring. It didn't work and the look on his face brought me back to my senses. I shouldn't have shouted at him. It was a knee-jerk reaction and I knew that I shouldn't have done it (I have forgiven myself).

Within a nano-second I knew that what was taking place was that my three-year-old son was growing. Not physically, but in trying to learn a new skill and pushing his boundary ever so slightly, his capacity to do things increased. Okay, it wasn't perfect, but he had achieved what he set out to do. It took courage for him to undertake the task and maybe next time he would overfill the cereal again, but over time he would of course understand what he needed to do to get it right.

"I'm doing it, daddy!"

If it's not perfect, keep trying

I learned a valuable lesson and it's one that we all need to remind ourselves of. If we expect to get things perfect the first few times we do something and then give it up as a bad job, none of us will ever come anywhere near to reaching our full potential.

THE iCAN CHRONICLES

iCAN...
BE A HAPPY
MOTHER

Elaine Hanzak-Gott

After the birth of our second child Ellis, my wife Helen went through a terrible bout of postnatal depression and it really pushed us both to the limit at times. What made it difficult back in 2006/7 was that my speaking schedule was getting busier and the engagements were happening further and further from home. This put even more pressure on things as neither of us had parents around to help, which usually happens when new children enter the world.

I bumped into a friend and fellow speaker, Clive Gott, while I was in the city centre and he asked how things were going. I didn't go into too much detail but told him that we were experiencing some pressures due to the second child coming along. I think he knew there was a bit more to it than that and he advised me that I should keep it all in check. He then gave me a phone number of a woman he knew that may be able to give us some advice. I called Elaine over the next few days and she did seem to understand exactly what we were going

iCan

through. It turned out that she knew only too well as she had been through much worse herself.

It seemed surreal standing in the pulpit. One of those "Am I really here?" moments. Yet I *was* there. A sea of expectant faces looking at me. Waiting for me to speak. After a shaky start I began my story. Thirteen years later that story is now being told worldwide and has begun to impact upon individuals, families, groups and even politics.

As a child I had an inbuilt desire to be a mother one day. I loved to play house and when my baby sister arrived when I was a ten-year-old she was my living doll. I adored her and loved to do all the essential care involved in bringing up a child. I was always a busy, capable and efficient girl and liked to be organised in whatever I did.

I became a teacher for children with severe learning difficulties and eventually married a colleague. Shortly after our wedding I was ecstatic to find that I was pregnant and approached the next nine months in my usual efficient manner. Although I did not really want to be a working mother, finances meant that I had to be – but I saw that everyone else managed so why couldn't I?

Sadly the pregnancy, birth and early days of motherhood were not the idyllic picture I had anticipated. I was physically poorly in the latter stages of pregnancy; I almost died giving birth and needed emergency surgery; the baby was born with the cord around his neck, but was fine; I had numerous problems with breastfeeding and even needed surgery again when baby Dominic was six weeks old. The week I was due back at my teaching post I spent in a children's ward with my son who had viral septicaemia! On top of all this Dominic was a very poor sleeper and I was mentally and physically exhausted but pretended to the world that I was all right – after all, I had everything I always wanted, so I could not complain, could I? I began to panic about what to make for meals. My mood swings were huge. I got anxious about daily tasks and forever seemed to have Dominic at the doctors for minor ailments. Eventually my GP said she felt I was suffering from postnatal depression. Who, me? I thought that mental illness affected the weaker members of society. Not someone like me who prided herself on being busy, efficient, organised. I was not a single mother living in a tiny flat managing on no support and little money. I felt I "had it all" – a comfortable home, a career I loved, a wonderful family, a baby I had yearned for. Why me? I felt ungrateful, guilty and very alone.

The weeks passed and I took antidepressants and attended a support group. However, due to the shame I felt as being seen as a bad mother (my false perception) I bottled up many of the negative feelings I was having. I painted on a mask of "I am fine" but in reality I was mentally unravelling. The week before the first Christmas as the mother I had longed to be I suffered a complete mental crisis. I wanted to hurt my son. I attacked my father and found ways to inflict wounds on myself. This developed as a way to make my mind focus – it just could not switch off or relax any more. Nine months of sleep deprivation, pressures of illness, life and a demanding new baby had all taken their toll on me. In the early hours of a wet December morning I was found curled up on a church doorway wearing just my nightgown.

I was admitted to a psychiatric hospital suffering from puerperal psychosis. This is a most extreme form of postnatal illness and affects 1 in 500 newly delivered mothers, often within hours of giving birth due to massive changes in

iCan

hormone levels. In my case I think it was all the stresses that basically built up in me until my mind and body said 'Enough'. I spent two months in what had been a Victorian asylum, without my baby. After various treatments, including medication, occupational therapy and electro-convulsive therapy I began to make a slow recovery. Baby Dominic was also put on the child protection register with Social Services as I had shaken him to stop him crying on his first Christmas Day when I had been allowed home for a few hours. It certainly was not the image I had carried for years of being a mother.

It took two more years of time, patience and treatment from all involved. My baby, husband, family, friends and colleagues had all been affected by my illness and most of all, me. Yet little by little I got back my confidence and desire to do the things I used to. At my worst I could not talk to one person let alone a group. Everyday tasks had been impossible and even deciding if I wanted tea or coffee was a decision that felt 'too much'. Yet recovery did come and one Sunday morning I noticed that the local church where I had gone to in my hours of deep crisis, were having a service for World Mental Health Day. I felt I should go. Members of the clergy and people from the health professions spoke about the stigma and ignorance surrounding mental illness. They commented on how people feel there is no way back from it; that once you have set off on that journey there is no way back.

Elaine's iCan moment #1

As I listened I got an urge which began in my toes and gradually worked its way up my body until I was tingling all over. It was as if someone or something was saying "Get up there girl!" So I did. I found myself walking up the aisle and asked the vicar, who knew me, if I could tell my story.

I took a deep breath and explained how two years earlier my life had fallen apart through mental illness. Yet here I was now back teaching and living my life as "normal" again. I said that mental illness can and does affect anyone – there is no "type" – but given treatment, time and support you *can* make a full recovery.

After the service I was approached by a member of staff from the local hospital who said she needed a service user to speak to a "few people" the following week about what had been good and what could have been better about their treatment. This time I felt very, very nervous as I had time to think about it. Part of my illness had zapped my self-confidence and many doubts and worries began to creep in. I decided I would at least try, and prepared a ten minute presentation. When I arrived at the hospital it was a full conference and I was seated on a platform on the top table. I nervously looked at the delegates. How on earth could I do it?

As I was being introduced I closed my eyes for a moment. The occupational therapist had taught me a technique of picturing a flickering flame at times of stress and breathing out so that the flame flickered. I did this and began to calm down.

Elaine's iCan moment #2
I was also telling myself "I can do this and when I have I will be better!" And I did. I reduced some delegates to tears and as I heard the rapturous applause, in my head I was punching the air! I did it!

That, I thought, was it. I was better. I had my darling, healthy son and I would go back just to living my life. However, from that event I was then invited to speak at a conference for hundreds of nurses in London later that year. I also managed to

iCan

do that. Each time I spoke someone said that I should write a book as it would help so many others. So I did. It took four years to be written, but finally in January 2005 *Eyes without Sparkle – a journey through postnatal illness* was published. Since then life has changed beyond recognition! As a result of the initial publicity I appeared on several national and local television programmes. The press also featured me in many articles and I was interviewed on various radio shows. I was asked to speak at conferences and give lectures to health profession students. I took a term off from my school teaching to explore the possibilities of this being a new career and have never looked back! At first I combined it with a sales job but in recent years I have concentrated full-time on my new role. Since I told my story many others have shared theirs with me. With their permission I can use other examples to help in my mission. I wrote my book and now speak about my experiences, primarily to offer hope to sufferers and their families. I also wanted to inspire them to show it is possible to make a full recovery from having almost been suicidal and unable to make the simplest of decisions. Through attending many conferences my knowledge has grown around the area too and I am now considered to be an 'Expert by Experience'.

I also aim to reduce the stigma and ignorance surrounding mental illness as I used to unfairly judge those affected by it and I wish to educate society to be more tolerant and understanding of sufferers. People generally are sympathetic and helpful to those with physical illness, so why not with a mental health issue? I feel this is especially relevant in the world of work where stigma and ignorance can prolong suffering as people feel they are being judged for 'faking illness'.

By informing people of some of the possible causes and early symptoms to look out for I hope to educate people to take preventive measures to help others. Another of my messages is to basically thank health professionals, as without their dedication people like me would not get their lives back. I am told that my talks are extremely moving, powerful and motivating.

During the last few years I have become involved in research in the area of postnatal illness; I represent many sufferers at a variety of conferences and at the Open University; my website is growing as a leading resource on the area; I have spoken in Australia and written articles in several publications. I have spoken to many health professionals and students; run workshops for those currently suffering and been an inspiration to attendees at support groups.

I have spoken at the European Parliament where issues of stigma I faced about employment and insurance are now being raised across the committees there. I have also been told that my story has literally saved lives as it has offered hope to those who had been contemplating suicide. I am humbled and proud to have been able to make that difference.

I am also a trustee of The Joanne (Joe) Bingley Memorial Foundation, set up after Joe sadly took her own life 10 weeks after giving birth to her daughter Emily. Through the charity I deliver workshops with fellow trustee Ann Girling, to professionals and parents, such as in Children's Centres. I am an expert at www.Greatvine.com where I offer support to those affected by postnatal illness. My blog and presentations are aimed at making life happier and easier for others.

iCan

My *iCan* moment was initially meant just for me. Yet the repercussions have been startling. Although my focus has been on postnatal illness I am told that I have inspired many of different ages, gender and experiences of mental distress. I feel that I was meant to do this – that my upbringing and skills acquired before I was ill, such as a confidence of public speaking and being empathic, were moulding me for the role I now have.

I now have a passion for helping others to prevent or at least lessen the suffering caused by mental illness, whether it is recognising early symptoms in loved ones or appealing for better resources and facilities within the health services. I felt a great sense of loss through suffering from puerperal psychosis. I lost out on early motherhood and the very special first few months of my baby son's life. I can never get them back. But I now know *iCan* help others to avoid and reduce the level of pain both myself and my family felt – and I shall strive to do so for as long as I am needed.

www.hanzak.com
http://www.joebingleymemorialfoundation.org.uk/

DIG DEEP

After my first talk for Samaritans they had me back for the following six years. My latest was to another 200 at the Annual Conference in York. Although I do enjoy doing a book signing afterwards, I was conscious that I had to drive all the way to Manchester to see one of my heroes, Deepak Chopra. I sold and signed so many books that I was 20 minutes late for his address. It was still amazing.

One of the most interesting things I heard him talk about was the notion that the Universe is actually us; we are the Universe, we are not in our body, but our bodies are in us. That the whole Universe is in us. Speaking in this way takes courage – there are many who would think this kind of talk ridiculous – but I firmly believe that there is far more to this world than we can fully explain.

In recent years some amazing and surreal things have happened in my life. One day I will definitely write about them, including finding the courage to forgive Mum's killer. Deepak's speech reminded me of a time when I was a young boy, soon after Mum had been murdered. I remember feeling so bad about what had happened to Mum, as well as all the other things that were taking place at home. But somehow I imagined that what I was experiencing was not real. It felt as if it was some kind of film or play and I was the observer. An observer watching everything that was taking place but that those things were not reality. I was reality. What was happening around me and to me was all being orchestrated. Having listened to Deepak I was taken back to that time. Although apparently there is no such thing as time.

Don't give up on your big dream

How different would life be if you knew that we are all part of the universe and that we are all connected and part of the same thing. Like the leaves of a tree, which fall to the ground and appear to be separate when they are, in fact, part of the whole. How different would life be if the things that we experienced were meant to happen in that precise way in order for each of us to get a glimpse of reality. The one which we struggle to recognise or to articulate.

Watch:
Glimpse of Reality with Richard McCann by Nic Askew
http://www.soulbiographies.com/films/a-glimpse-of-reality/

WATCH

Glimpse of Reality
with Richard McCann by Nic Askew

www.soulbiographies.com/films/a-glimpse-of-reality/

MAKE YOUR MIND UP

Do I stay or do I go? It was quite a dilemma. I had just got off the train at Kings Norton station near Birmingham. It was around 15 minutes' walk from the station to the venue where I was speaking around an hour later. It was one of those smaller stations that don't have a taxi rank outside but I did notice a bus stop over the road from the station. I found out from someone in the queue that I needed the 45 bus to get to where I wanted to be.

My dilemma was that, according to the timetable, the buses from this stop would arrive between every 7–10 minutes. The longest I would have to wait was 10 minutes and with the 4-minute bus ride I would arrive at the venue in no more than 14 minutes. I tried to work out what my best course of action would be. Do I stop and wait? Or do I get some well-needed exercise? I didn't want to start walking and then have the bus arrive and sail past me with all those that were in the queue looking on laughing at me.

iCan

You may have been there yourself at one time or another. I don't mean faced with a dilemma about walking or not (although you may have been), but you have probably been faced with something that requires you have to make a decision. It may be whether you go to university or not, do you try to become an actor or a writer, do you continue putting up with this uncaring boss or do you go off and work for yourself? We are continually faced with decisions, and in my experience many people decide not to do anything.

So I made my move and yes, you guessed it, 5 minutes later the bus passed me. I turned around as it passed, and I smiled. Not to those who had seen me decide to walk, but to myself.

Be decisive

This was a great example of what I believe we all should do when faced with a crossroads. Be decisive. If you need some time to think it through then do that, but act quickly. Don't procrastinate. Just do something and accept what happens. It's better than doing nothing. Whatever the outcome, know you gave it your best. If you need to reflect on the decision in the future and adjust your plans, that's fine – but keep the momentum going.

So I could have got there 7–8 minutes earlier, but I would not have got the exercise and I would not have had the material to write this piece.

What is it that you are in two minds to do? Write it down here and if you have more than one write them all. Be decisive and write down when you will do it or put a line through it and decide not to do it. Live with the outcome, but whatever you do, do something.

1 ....

2 ....

3 ....

ACHIEVEMENT BEGINS WITH A GOAL

DECIDE AND IT WILL HAPPEN

Things don't happen by accident, unless you are the one in a million who achieves things by being in the right place at the right time or winning the lottery or inheriting a lot of money. Most of us achieve things in life by deciding to achieve something.

In June 2002, while at work I received one of the calls that I had always been dreading. It was Angela, my younger sister, informing me that Sonia, my sister, had stabbed her boyfriend and had been arrested. It had been a very turbulent relationship and after a weekend of violence she picked up a knife and stabbed him in self-defence. After she was released and she told me what had happened I decided that day to write about our life. About how Mum's death had affected us and how we had been dealt one of those blows in life that would be felt for generations. It was almost 30 years after Mum's death and I could see that both these events were somehow related. I thought to myself that if I wrote a book about our lives then maybe Sonia would get a reduced prison sentence. I had to do something and maybe it was a little naïve of me, as writing a book was never going to influence the criminal justice system. The very important point is that I did not have to wait until she did that. I could have written it a year before the incident, a month before or the night before. The potential to write it was always there. I could have written it at any time. *It happened because I decided it would happen.* It's as easy as that.

The book went on to be a number one bestseller and I began to receive invitations to speak about my extraordinary life to audiences around the UK. In my first year I only spoke three times from the stage and in my second year it was 11. Although I was getting busier this kind of rate wasn't going to get me very far. During my second year (2006) you may recall that I told you earlier (page 16) that I met W. Mitchell at a conference, and days later I walked away from university to take up speaking full time. After two years of speaking, and now with a family to provide for things were getting serious. I needed to do something and fast.

First I spent some time with a lady called Jane Kenyon, a coach who helped me think about where I might take my speaking. We had four sessions together. In the final session she asked me to think about what I would like to achieve in the future.

In five minutes I had to write down a list of things I would love to achieve if only I had a magic wand. I wrote down 34 things. Six years later, I still have the piece of paper, except now there are 20 things highlighted because I have achieved them.

In the same year I was shown a film called *The Secret*, which many of you will have seen. It's become a bit of a legendary film in the personal development world. The concept is that whatever it is you want to achieve, you can attract it simply by believing it will happen. That you send out a vibration and the universe will answer by giving you what you think about. I think there is a little more to it than that. You have to take some action – no matter how long you sit in your chair waiting for something to appear, it won't come unless you take a few action steps to help it, which is why I have included the action steps throughout the book.

One thing I took away from *The Secret* was that we need an image for the thing we wanted to achieve, for example a house, a car, or a cheque for a large sum of money we wanted to earn. I actually wrote out a cheque for the amount of money I wanted to earn and post-dated the cheque for 12 months' later. I placed it in my wallet so that I could focus on it. That year I also had a goal to speak at 50 events, which was far more than the 11 from the previous year. I went on to speak 78 times that year and earn within 5% of what was on the cheque. I also placed a screensaver on my laptop for the car I wanted to drive (a silver BMW) and I made sure that I drove one to get emotionally connected with achieving it. My good friend Stuart Howarth had one at the time. I now drive the very same car that I had on my PC. I have written the third book that was on my list too. In fact you have it in your hand, unless of course you are reading the electronic version. There are more, but I think I have made my point.

iCan

Miracles will happen

Our brains are super-computers; they will work out a way of achieving it. Decide what it is you want from life and believe that you can achieve it. For me with the speaking I had an enormous reason to make it happen. It had to work. I had to make a success of it. I didn't want my daughter to go without like I did as a child. You need a big enough WHY and then miracles will happen in your life. The thing is, they are not miracles at all. It's just the way it is. Now you know there are no excuses for not achieving what you truly desire. It's there waiting for you.

If you had a magic wand and you could have anything that you liked then what would it be? Remember I wrote out 34 and I have achieved 20 of them now. What might happen if you were to write out your own list if you thought you would definitely achieve more than half of them?

Write your list here:

1 ....

2 ....

3 ....

4 ....

5 ....

6 ....

7 ....

8 ....

9 ....

10...

11...

12...

12...

14...

15...

16...

17...

18...

19...

20...

21...

22...

23...

24...

25...

26...

27...

28...

29...

30...

The Secret
Rhonda Byrne
Simon & Schuster, 2006

iCan

THE iCAN CHRONICLES

iCAN...
NOW

Wendy Swanson

Paralyzed with a devastating attack from multiple sclerosis I lay daily on my couch wondering what was going to happen to me next. I couldn't walk and sitting up was a major chore. Weakness invaded my limbs and my husband and children were waiting on me hand and foot. Pain wracked my body while bladder and bowel function were lost. Silence was my friend now.

A few short months before I had been working, helping out with my new granddaughter and running all over town shopping, paying bills and taking care of my family, including my in-laws. Music, laughter and dance were my joys in those days. A diagnosis was given of multiple sclerosis and a long, slow recuperation began. Medications and finally mega steroids were used to get my body back into some form of working order. Nursing and homecare were brought in to help me when my husband and children returned to work and school while I tried to figure out what to do. For the next three years we worked on making a new life with my illness now included in it.

Wendy's iCan moment #1

When I was alone and in the silence I craved, I prayed to God to show me what to do. I received a blessing of His peace.
"You can pray for others now, my grace is sufficient for you", He said.

And it was. Many people came into our home with needs that I would pray for. I made up a God's Box for special intentions and people would call or come over and we would place their messages inside. I prayed every day on the box for the needs of others. Somehow taking the focus off of myself and thinking about others' troubles always made my own circumstances appear small.

One of the special ladies who came to take care of me was an old friend. It was a joy to see her every week – she was very positive and uplifting. She encouraged me to remember all the things that were happening in my life and to do something with them for others with MS. I made herbal potpourri for Christmas one year and she encouraged me to write down the recipe. I was researching organic foods and good nutrition in order to change my diet. She told me to do something with all the knowledge I was obtaining.

These hints were coming all the time but I was not ready to put them into action. I kept asking God:

"What am I supposed to do now?"

And He kept answering, "Pray"

So I kept on praying. Each year I would get stronger and stronger. I started out with a wheelchair, then to a walker and then to a cane. Every Monday morning for about five years I would try and jump out of bed like I used to and walk quickly to the bathroom. Gradually things were getting better and

iCan

better. Every night when he kissed me goodnight my husband would say "Please get better so you can cook again." We started cooking together and became closer than ever. I was housebound but joined the MS Society and started working on fundraising for a cure.

Wendy's iCan moments

It was at this time I was seeing a social worker who encouraged me to set attainable goals. I asked her how long it would take to set an attainable goal at my level of recuperation and she said "one year." I decided to make a cookbook to sell for MS. It took me one year. Then the next year I decided to do a second edition. It took me one year. Now I am working on my final copy. It will take me one year. I became a volunteer for World Vision through training on the internet. It took me one year.

Now I go out whenever I can and speak about child sponsorship. I decided to start a web-based business. It took me one year. We now have a successful business, which is five years old. I decided to put on a variety show for charity. The planning took one year. I did this for three years in a row with the help of family and friends and raised money and awareness for our local shelter.

Recently I was awarded the YMCA Peace Medallion for my work in the community and have been placed on the Mayor's Honour List. All this, and I am just now able to leave my home more frequently. There is nothing that cannot be overcome with the help of God. iCan do all things through Christ who strengthens me and could have done none of this without His grace working in my life. I am grateful for the new life I have and all He has given me.

SET A GOAL - THEN DOUBLE IT

Soon after I had written on the cheque how much I wanted to receive, I joined my very first mastermind group. This is a group of people who get together a few times a year to share goals, ideas, receive support and generally help each other move forward. One of our members was a speaker called Martin Goodyer, who introduced me to another concept that changed how I thought of goal-setting. When I told them my financial goal for that particular year Martin suggested that I was limiting myself by having that goal and that I should double it. It felt foolish as the goal was already far more than I had ever earned in a conventional job but this was someone whom I trusted so I did double it. The remarkable thing was that by the time 12 months had passed from the time I set the new goal I achieved it. In fact only four months after I set the goal I achieved the monthly equivalent of the annual goal.

iCan

Maybe I am one of the lucky one in a million, but I think not. One way of thinking about it is that if I asked you to write down now a way of raising £50 for a good cause it would not be too difficult to come up with a few ideas. You could probably achieve it by taking part in your local half marathon. You could set up a car boot sale and get rid of a load of clutter out of your loft. Whatever you decide you could probably do it quite easily.

What if I then thanked you for your kind donation of £50 but went on to explain that there had been a disaster and we now needed to raise £2,000? I'd ask you to think of ways in which you could achieve this much larger amount. You'd then have to come up with other, more creative ways to do it. You might come up with a gala dinner where you could sell tables and ask for people to donate prizes that could be auctioned on the night. I think that would just about do it. Ten tables at £400 a table minus room hire would probably generate £2,000. You may even raise slightly more. The point is that when I asked you to raise £50 your brain did not come up with the creative £2,000 idea. Its only when you have that goal does your brain come up with it.

Put pictures on your dream board

It will not be a coincidence if you spend some time to think about what you want to achieve this year and write them down and you then achieve them. You could go one step further, as my good friend Molly Harvey often recommends, and have a dream board in the house (you should see hers). Put pictures of what you want to achieve on that board and expect to achieve it. If it's your goal to earn £18,000 a year you are likely only to get the qualifications for a £18,000 job. When you look through the recruitment section of the local paper or online you will only see vacancies that are around £18,000.

If your goal is to speak 20 times a year, when you get to 18 talks you are likely to stop looking for much longer. Whatever your goal, double it. Martin shared a simple process with us. Make the goal larger than you may have thought possible. Look around and realise that others achieve such levels of success. Know that you can, too. Then you can let the universe do its work. (not forgetting to play your part by taking whatever action your mind suggests you take)

I truly hope that you have that list of goals compiled really soon and that you let me know when those apparent miracles begin happening, and they will – trust me.

A few years ago Simon Weston, the Falklands hero, suggested I call a speaker agency called Abingdon Management who looked after most of his work, so I called them but they were not interested. So I printed out their web page, which featured the speakers they had who spoke about overcoming adversity, and I stuck on my photo as though I was one of their speakers. I focused on it for over a year. Of course this was not going to work so after some more experience and when the opportunity arose I called them again and invited them to see me in action. They loved me and took me on.

iCan

"You can do it, son"

CHOOSE GOALS WITH MEANING

It was my son Ellis's first sports day at nursery and I was so thankful that I was able to rearrange a meeting so that I could be there to watch him. There weren't many Dads there, as I imagine most were unable to get the time off work.

So there I was, camera charged ready to film my only son's first major achievement. This was going to be one of those days that I would remember for years, or so I thought. Having checked the board with the names and events on, I quickly worked out that he only had two events. First it was the beanbag race followed by the running race. I had quite forgotten that a beanbag race ever existed. For those of you who have also forgotten, you put a small square bag full of beans on your head, and you have to run without dropping it (quite a skill I might add).

iCan

So there they were, the young athletes in their yellow T-shirts, except my son Ellis who refused to wear his, lined up at the start. I gave him the fatherly team talk: "You can do it, son." I think it was more for me than for him. I switched the camera to shoot mode and made my way to the finish line with all the other parents who had just given the same talk to each of their children. The stakes were high, but with all this talk of 'iCan' in our house I was sure some of it had rubbed off on Ellis, even though he wasn't quite three yet.

"On your marks … get set … GO!" and they were gone … that is, except Ellis. He just froze and didn't seem to know what to do. My heart sank. I turned to my wife and we grimaced. "Bless him," she said. All the other children were well past half-way before he had even worked in which direction to head. I'm afraid this wasn't going to be one of those *Chariots of Fire* moments with the enormous comeback that would be required to come out with any of the three medals available. He walked the whole distance, and he soon worked out that he was last. We could see he was fighting back the tears as he approached the line (I can feel the emotion as I type this). We both threw our arms around him and congratulated him on completing the race. Then we headed over to the refreshment table for a juice and a hankie.

We still had the running race for Ellis to take part in and I thought "surely he's not going to come last in both his events." Twenty minutes later the names for the running race were called out and I once again took him over to the start line. I knelt down beside him and began giving him the McCann team talk again. I knew it was an uphill battle, but I had to give it my best shot. I told him that if he was the fastest over the line that he could have as much mango as he wanted (he loves dried mango). We were told to get our children into position. "On your marks … get set … GO!"

Off they all went and thankfully there was no one left on the start line. That was already an improvement from the first race, so I was happy. The camera was rolling, the children were running and the parents were all cheering. And Ellis, my son was, er … winning. He was half a stride in front of the only other person near him who seemed to be closing fast. Closing even faster was the finish line. Now it was my turn to get emotional as I saw my son stride through the tape on the finish line with young Timmy hot on his heels. Less than a second separated them, but it didn't matter. Ellis was first. He had exceeded all our expectations and come out a gold medal winner in the end. I was incredibly proud. Again we both got down on our knees and threw our arms around him.

"Can I have my mango now?" he asked.

Access your inner reserves

I hadn't expected him to win, so I didn't have any mango. I just knew that if I offered him something that meant a lot to him, he might just be able to access those inner reserves that we all have to do more than we are currently doing. Despite explaining this on a regular basis as a motivational speaker, I had no idea that it would be so successful on my two-year-old son.

Now, I'm not suggesting that you go out and buy yourself a packet of dried mango, but a goal that means something to you is much more likely to be achieved than one with no meaning. You need a big enough Why. Why am I going for this promotion? What might it do for me? Why am I going to leave

iCan

the so called security of this 9 to 5 job and set up my own small business? Why am I donating my kidney to a family member who might die otherwise? When you have a goal and the reason is meaningful enough you will do everything in your power to make it happen. Don't take my word for it, ask Ellis.

Take just three of your goals and write them here and then underneath write WHY it's important for you to achieve that goal. Big enough reasons WHY allow us to access those inner reserves we have floating around inside.

Goal 1...

Why?...

....

....

Goal 2...

Why?...

....

....

Goal 3...

Why?...

....

....

THE iCAN CHRONICLES

DADDY...
iCAN

David Bradley

I received this story from a reader I initially heard from some years ago when my first book was published. He heard about this book through my regular newsletter. A very inspirational story it is too.

I always remember the day we found out that our daughter Georgia, now 15, was going to be born with spina bifida. We always had to bring our son Brandon, who is autistic, along with us for the antenatal sessions as we had nobody we could leave him with. At the time he was just five. Normally I had to walk around the grounds of the hospital with him while my wife Lorna was inside as Brandon was at that time very fearful of buildings and crowds, but he later overcame this.

Anyway, on this occasion Brandon, who at that time was severely speech impaired, seemed to sense that something was wrong and he surprised me by pulling me towards the hospital entrance. We went to the scanning room and Lorna was at that moment undergoing a scan. She was beaming with the news she had just been given that we were getting a girl – we had been hoping for a girl.

Georgia standing tall despite the spina bifida she was born with.

Within moments her smiles turned to tears, shock and panic. We were told that our child would be born with spina bifida and the implications were explained to us, from the scenario that she would be likely to be wheelchair bound to the possibility that our baby may not even survive the birth. Lorna's despair broke my heart and while I too felt despair, I had to appear to be strong for her sake. My own tears had to be shed quietly when I was alone, such as driving the car home from work.

However, I always believe in the power of positive thinking. It is not always easy to apply though! On that day in August 1996 I insisted to Lorna that in spite of the news we had received, life should and would continue normally. We went out that evening to buy baby clothes (something we had planned to do anyway) and as an act of faith that Georgia would walk I bought her a pair of baby shoes! Our impending holiday proceeded as planned – there would have been nothing to gain in cancelling it.

Within a few days we went to a place of spiritual retreat and Lorna received a special 'mother's blessing'. After she received that blessing, subsequent scans revealed no deterioration of the lesion which caused Georgia's condition. The doctors had told us that we could expect it to increase in size as the pregnancy continued. But it never did.

When Georgia was born the doctors were very cautiously optimistic. They warned us not to set our hopes too high, that they could not guarantee that she would walk. She might and might not, they said.

iCan

Determination was something I sensed in Georgia the very moment she was born. A natural birth was too risky, so she was born by caesarean section. For a baby of only 5lb 10 oz. she had such a loud cry, which expressed determination and a very definite iCan attitude! This has been realised in her success not only in walking but dancing beautifully and cycling, too. She has a condition that we have to watch very carefully, but her doctors consider her to be a remarkable child and so do we.

David and Georgia's iCan moment

I was quite ashamed when, a few years back, she asked me to remove the stabilisers on her cycle. I did so with reluctance and much caution, thinking she would not be able to balance, and to my shame I told her so. But Georgia knew best.

She said, "Daddy, I Can".

And she was right! She rides her cycle without them and without difficulty. She is also a beautiful dancer and while her childhood has not been without health scares and anxious moments – at three months of age she had to have a shunt inserted for hydrocephalus, to drain fluid from the brain, and this led to epilepsy – Georgia has fought everything bravely and without any self-pity. She has been an example to us, her parents. It is Georgia who has taught us to say "iCan" and she always displays humility - never pride - using, in the special school she attends, her breakthroughs to show caring towards and encourage other children who may be experiencing difficulties. It is Georgia who has taught us to say *"iCan."*

JIM'LL FIX IT

In July 2010 I discovered that Peter Sutcliffe would remain behind bars for the rest of his life as his High Court appeal against his whole life tariff was unsuccessful. Sky News interviewed me live outside a venue I had spoken at a few minutes earlier, and believe me, it was definitely outside my comfort zone. While I was there I spent some time chatting with the lovely reporter Tessa Chapman who was interested in how I became a motivational speaker. She asked me for some advice as she was to give a presentation to a college in a few weeks' time. After I had shared a few ideas, I asked her a few questions.

I was intrigued at how she became a presenter for Sky News. What she then told me I thought was fantastic, and I wanted to share it with you. When she was six years of age she wrote to *Jim'll Fix It*. For my younger readers I should explain that this was a weekly programme presented by the late Sir Jimmy Savile, a Radio DJ and TV celebrity. Members of the public wrote to Jim and asked him for help to achieve a dream or ambition they had. He chose half a dozen on each show from the 20,000 he was sent each week, to help fulfill their dreams.

iCan

Tessa Chapman achieved her dream to be a news reporter

Tessa had some idea where she wanted to be in the future and it was something that was meaningful to her. She had wanted to read the news for most of her life, and some might call it luck that she did indeed get to read the news, despite being unsuccessful with Jimmy Savile, but I would suggest that it's more than that. When we know what we want to be, do, or achieve, our brain is on heightened alert to look for ways in which we can make it a reality.

If you rang up for a pizza and the pizza shop owner asked what type of pizza you wanted I doubt you would reply with 'Don't know' or 'Surprise me'. But that is what happens for many people. They go through life not knowing where they want to be and they stop in a job they hate for 15 years.

I met a woman in York who had sat in on one of my talks, and afterwards she told me a story of being made redundant after working for BT for years. She soon discovered that it was a blessing in disguise, as she wasn't fulfilled in her job and she now works with the local authority helping young people who may have had issues to deal with in their life. She's never been happier.

Dear Jim...

If you were to write to Jim'll Fix It, what would you ask for? Go on, write it here instead.

Then write another, this time from Jim telling you that the show ended 20 years ago, but here's what you need to do to achieve that thing. You'll be surprised what you might come up with.

iCan

Dear Jim, could you please fix it for me to:

....

....

....

....

....

....

Now then, as it happens, to really achieve that you really should start by doing this:

....

....

....

....

....

....

BELIEVE IT WILL HAPPEN

It was finally time for Skye, our daughter, to go to 'big school' as we knew it. Actually it was primary school, but after two years at nursery, it felt like big school to us and to Skye. It probably did to you too, when you first went. Like a lot of parents we went to visit the schools in the local area to see which one we thought was best for our precious daughter.

In one of the schools we visited, we came across something very interesting on the wall of one of the classrooms. *A Hope Wall*. This I just had to see. What I found on the wall were around 30 small booklets that the children had made and stuck on the wall. These booklets looked like passports – as you opened each one, there was an illustration of the child and then a message on the opposite page. In the future I hope … "to own a big house" said one, "to work with young people", "to have a family", "to be successful" and on they all went. Very sweet, I thought. There was nothing like this at my school. How fantastic, until I thought about it a little more. Hope is great and we must all hope for various things. I hope to live

iCan

until I am 100, I hope to live long enough to see my grandchildren, I hope one day to have this book published. Or do I?

I have been hoping to publish this book for around three years. Nothing happened. I had started it a few times but no, hoping it would be out into print didn't make it happen. It happened because I decided that '*I Will*' write and publish this book. We can hope to pass our exams and that might work, we can hope to pass our driving lesson and that might work too. We can hope the dentist knows what he is doing when he next fills our tooth. Of course he knows what he's doing. "I *will* pass my driving lesson" is something different to "I hope to pass it." When you say that you will do something it has a different energy to "I *hope* to do something." It's like saying "I *might* write a book" or "I *might* marry you."

Commit to your goals

When I decided to become a speaker in 2006 I didn't say that I might become one, that I hope that it works out, that if it doesn't work out I will try something else. I knew that this was going to work and that I would do whatever it took to make it happen. The rest is history. Live in hope if you want – in some cases, that's what we need to be feeling. I hope one day that they find a cure for cancer. But when it comes to accomplishments, that you want to achieve, commit to achieving them. Believe it will happen and you will be surprised what the universe will do for you.

Write 3 things that you have not committed to achieving and do so in the positive.

e.g. I will publish this book in 2012.

1. ....
2. ....
3. ....

In fact let's go one step further.

For each of your goals that you have now committed to achieve, write down how it feels to have achieved them.

e.g. It feels amazing to have finally been able to publish my 3rd book. Not forgetting to try and imagine how it will feel to achieve the goal. And feel it.

1. ....
2. ....
3. ....

iCan

THE iCAN CHRONICLES

DON'T TELL ME THAT I CAN'T BECAUSE... iCAN...

Steve Wilkinson

Steve was the second person I came across who spoke from the stage in a wheelchair. I first met him at an event while in the car park. I could see him manoeuvring around his car to get his wheelchair from inside the back of it. It looked a bit of a struggle and I offered him some help. He declined and I made my way into the hotel. He followed me in a minute or two later. He's now become a friend and the things he gets up to despite his condition inspire me. I find myself wondering just what he will try next.

Reflecting on my life in recent years, I've realised I've been operating the iCan philosophy since my childhood. Born with spina bifida in the early 50s, I spent a lot of the first eight years of my life in hospital or attending out patients for surgery and treatment to stabilise my condition. Although I now use a wheelchair most of the time, dealing with my disability has never held me back.

Starting Pendower Hall School in Newcastle in 1961, a special school for disabled kids, I showed that a delayed start to full-time education was not a problem and three years later, I passed the 11+ exam. At first, the authorities said I couldn't go to the local grammar school as they said I wouldn't be able to manage. *How wrong could they be?*

My parents' determination to urge them to give me a trial was rewarded as my *iCan* attitude showed through. I coped admirably and fitted in like any other pupil. Seven years later, I left with O and A levels to go to Newcastle University, where I graduated with a BSc in mathematics.

My working life of 30 years in the IT industry was littered with successes of which I'm very proud. People and organisations have benefited from what *iCan* do for them. Starting as a computer programmer, I progressed into management and consultancy positions, including a five year period where I demonstrated *iCan* also run my own business helping organisations of all sizes benefit from their computer systems.

Outside work, I enjoy sharing a happy private life with my wife, Judith, and stepson, Matthew. *iCan* travel the world holidaying with them, as *iCan* cope with the complexities of air travel, although I have had cause to take legal action under the Disability Discrimination Act against one airline, which I won.

ACHIEVEMENT BEGINS WITH A GOAL

The complex process involved in this case motivated me to campaign for changes in the legislation to make it easier for other disabled people. I am confident *iCan* make a difference, but I need more support from others to demonstrate that they, too, can successfully challenge those who have little or no respect for disabled people.

Steve's iCan moments #1

Once I recognised that I had this iCan attitude to life, I started to push the boundaries and showed that iCan take on challenges outside my comfort zone, raising money for charity at the same time. Since mid-2007, I've abseiled from the Tyne Bridge, demonstrating iCan overcome my fear of heights, showed iCan walk on hot coals at 1200 degrees centigrade – on my hands – and soared to 200 feet parasailing behind a speedboat for a lengthy 25 minutes.

Throughout my life, I've always had an attitude that if someone says to me "you can't do that", I'm inspired to challenge their opinion and show that *iCan*. To me, their view is like waving a red rag to a bull.

This situation first occurred when my parents were told I couldn't cope at the grammar school. My determination to prove the authorities wrong was rewarded with the exam and career successes that followed.

More recently, when I first applied to abseil from the Tyne Bridge, I was naturally apprehensive about going out of my comfort zone in this daunting way, so when the organisers said I couldn't take part, I could easily have accepted their response as an excuse. But that's not the WheelchairSteve way! I was determined to find a way to show them they were wrong.

iCan

It's ironic, but the problem was not the descent from the bridge. The difficulty, for me, was getting over the four-foot barrier at the edge of the bridge to the ledge from which the abseil takes place. The organisers said they would need scaffolding – so I tracked down the scaffolding!

As it happened, we weren't able to acquire the scaffolding in time for the event, but I was told an abseil event for Disability North to be held later in the year had already organised to have scaffolding, and that was how I eventually took part in the abseil.

Steve's iCan moments #2

I think it's interesting to note in both the abseil and the parasail events, the complexities are in the set up. Getting down the steps of the pier on to the speedboat, which I did by shuffling on my backside, and being attached to the parachute, achieved by two people lifting me while being clipped on, were two challenges my iCan attitude helped me to overcome.

Once descending the 80 feet to the River Tyne on the abseil rope or soaring above the Humber at two hundred feet, my disability temporarily disappeared as I carried out those activities no differently to how anyone else would – and it was a great feeling.

Now I've learnt *iCan* earn a living as a speaker, as people are inspired by listening to how I've dealt with my disability, seeing what I've achieved in my life, and learning from how *iCan* overcome the obstacles put before me.

For the future, I know *iCan* make a difference in the world and leave a legacy, with regard to how disability is perceived. I've demonstrated *iCan* overcome the constraints society places on me due to my physical limitations and do things not expected of someone in a wheelchair.

It is a fact that everyone will encounter disability at some time in their life, either personally, through friends or family, and in places where they work or spend leisure time. You must adopt the *iCan* philosophy in these situations.

If it is you who becomes disabled, I urge you to adopt my approach to life and focus on the aspects of life where you can continue to say *iCan* rather than the opposite. Life won't be the same, but it's certainly far from over. Decide what you want to do, decide *iCan* do it, and you'll find a way.

If it is someone else with a disability you encounter, you should decide *iCan* consider this person to be capable of much more than may at first be apparent. The key is to appreciate the world from their point of view, which is best achieved by communicating with them. But it is vital you decide *iCan* communicate on a level that doesn't make assumptions about how life is disabling them. Treat them as you would want to be treated. Patronising talk still happens and must be a big "No, no!"

And that, in a nutshell, is the Steve "WheelchairSteve" Wilkinson story so far. There's a lot more yet to be achieved. I trust my insight into how the *iCan* philosophy has had, and still has, a positive impact on my life will inspire you as a result of reading this short story. If *"iCan"*, so can you!

www.wheelchairsteve.com

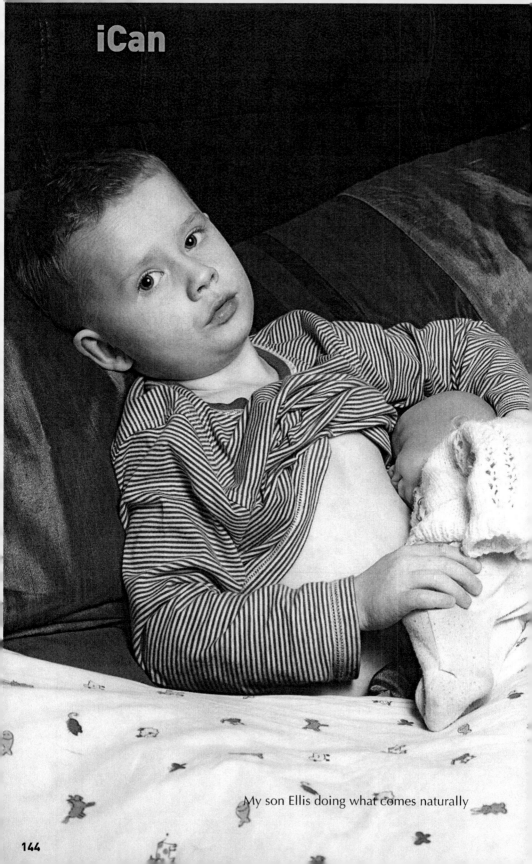

My son Ellis doing what comes naturally

IF THEY CAN DO IT, YOU CAN

The evening started out as quite normal. My wife had taken the two girls out for a walk. Ellis, my two-year-old son, was upstairs playing noisily with some toys. Then the noise suddenly stopped. I was OK for a minute or two until I got that sinking feeling. If you're a parent, you'll know the kind of feeling that parents get when they fear one of their brood has come to some harm. I rushed upstairs, with my senses on high alert, and I into our bedroom.

My son was sitting on the bed, alone, and wrapped around his waist was a cushion: a feeding cushion. On it he had placed a doll. I rushed in so quickly that he didn't even notice my stealth-like actions, so I bounced back out and ran downstairs to get the family camera. I just had to get a photo of this.

Ellis hadn't moved an inch and this gave me the perfect opportunity to take this picture. It's one I am sure to show at his wedding.

iCan

Yes, if you haven't worked it out yet, he is breastfeeding his sister's doll. I had to stop myself from laughing hysterically as I didn't want to hurt his young feelings.

Wash off the conditioners

"Why was he doing this?" you might ask. Well, like most of us in life, we are influenced by what goes on around us. We often replicate the things that those around us do. We often get conditioned to behave, believe or think in a certain way. Or, conversely, we don't do the things that those around us never have. If our parents have never been to university, we can be fooled into believing that it's beyond us, too. I was brought up, like many, on various council estates. For many years, I thought that those who owned their own homes were better than me. If no-one in your family has owned their own business or worked for themselves then who are we to think we can (some might think)?

Well, like all conditioners, they are there to be washed off and that's exactly what we should do. What may you have been exposed to over the years and how might that have distorted your view of just what you are capable of? Never forget how miraculous you are.

BREAK YOUR SPEED LIMIT

I was on my way to speak for a housing association and I hadn't left myself as much time to get there as I would normally. I always try to leave myself at least an hour's leeway in case of incidents that might slow me down.

You know what happens when you don't leave yourself enough time. You get stuck behind a delivery van with one of those pesky stickers advising the annoyed traffic that there is no way on this earth that the vehicle in front of you can achieve anything more than 56, 60 or even 70 miles an hour – whichever the management has decided as the limit for their untrustworthy drivers. This particular driver could go no faster than 70mph. I shouldn't complain as it is the national speed limit here in the UK, but you know how it is. 72 or 73 isn't too bad, and it could just help me make up a few minutes of lost time – but not on this occasion.

Get off the road to nowhere

What I find astonishing is that there are thousands of folks limiting themselves in life. They might as well have had someone else decide whether or not they take part in the slow lane of life or the metaphorical superhighway. I know that we all need to slow down at some point and take some time out for ourselves, but come on! If you have been forced into the slow lane of life where nothing much happens, where people limit just what they get involved in, where achievements are small: take the slip road that's waiting for you. Get off the road to nowhere. *Start heading for somewhere and real soon.* I dare you to break what you might have considered a speed limit in the past. It's where the magic is.

*Please note that the author does not encourage, endorse nor involve himself in breaking whatever speed limit applies in your neck of the woods. However on the 3rd Sept 1995 20:05hrs he did drive at 42mph in a 30mph zone and received 3points on his licence, which he is pleased to announce have now expired. He has now learned his lesson.

ACHIEVEMENT BEGINS WITH A GOAL

iCan

NEVER
GIVE UP

PUT THE EFFORT IN

Achievement does begin with a goal. But things don't come easy. If only it were as simple as setting a goal and achieving it. As I grew up, my only real goal was that one day I would have the kind of life that many of my classmates enjoyed. Warm, secure homes full of love and a happy family. I now have this in my life but it has taken me a half a life time to get here so it definitely didn't happen overnight. This is true of most achievements.

If you don't put the effort in, you won't get anything back.

There were many times that I thought about giving up, but I am I so glad that I never went ahead with any of my thoughts of ending my life. They began before Mum's killer was caught, so I was not even 10 years of age.

To imagine any of my children considering taking their life breaks my heart. But when I think about the countless others who have given up on something else in life it also breaks my heart. I'm sure we all know someone who has started something, a diet, keep fit routine, or their own business and has given up on it. As President of The Professional Speaking Association of my local region I have seen many speakers

iCan

come and go. I have seen some throw the towel in after a year trying to break into the speaking arena. I'm talking about individuals with talent too.

Earlier I mentioned getting my first speaking engagement in 2005 and that year I only spoke 3 times. Should I have given up? Some may have given up but I kept on ploughing ahead. The following year was a total of 11 engagements and although I was becoming busier, it certainly wasn't enough to pay the bills and feed and clothe my newly arrived daughter, Skye. I kept going because I knew that there were others out there with stories less powerful than my own and I knew that if I just kept at it, getting slightly better each time, growing, improving while all the time being seen by more and more people, the snowball would eventually gain some momentum. Even in my third year it started off a little better, but with 10 engagements in the first 3 months with less than a £1,000 earned you would have completely understood if I had thrown the towel in at that point.

But I didn't, and believe me, it took some courage not to do so. It was what Darren Hardy, a speaker from America, describes as *The Compound Effect*. Small incremental changes are hardly noticeable from one day to the next, but over time they compound together and we eventually see massive changes. He asked, in a presentation I saw him deliver, whether or not we would like £1 million today or 1p that would be doubled every day for 31 days. I was amazed that if you chose the million, you would in fact come off worse. 1p doubled every day after 20 days was only £5,242 – nothing like the £1 million but after day 31 it was an amazing £10,737,418 – a great example of what can happen over time if you just hang on in there.

For me and my speaking there was absolutely no turning back for me. What would people have said? I had tried and failed. No way. And now it's become a full time career for me and I have become one of the busiest speakers in the UK. I have now delivered over a thousand presentations / workshops / motivational days in five years. The rest is history.

Moving forward

What small steps in the right direction do you need to be making? Are you prepared to keep moving forward in the right direction and have you enough courage to keep going when there is no real evidence that you are going to succeed? To achieve any sort of success you need to serve your apprenticeship. That's where the foundations are laid.

Never give up.

The Compound Effect

Darren Hardy

Dream Builders, 2010

iCAN...
BOUNCE
BACK

Michael Bunting

I was working as a police officer at Millgarth Police Station, Leeds, when on 24 August 1997 I was sent to a job that would change my life forever.

The report was that there was a violent incident ongoing at an address in a notorious part of the city. When I arrived, I was violently assaulted by one of the men, who was heavily in drink. He held me down by my shirt collar and repeatedly punched me in the head and face in a sustained attack. I lost part of my right upper tooth, damaged my left eye socket (resulting in partial loss of vision for several weeks afterwards) and received cuts and bruises all to my head, face and mouth. My assailant was eventually restrained by colleagues and he was arrested, charged and convicted for assaulting me. I was compensated.

A year later, I was charged with assault for the force I'd used to defend myself. My assailant was completely uninjured. A further year later I was convicted of common assault after being controversially charged with this offence during my trial (23 months after the incident). I was sent to prison for four months in legally unprecedented circumstances. It was the worst possible outcome for me as a serving policeman.

My time in prison compounded the stress, dejection and betrayal of the previous two years. I was repeatedly beaten and injured and subjected to torturous mental abuse, bullying and threats. I was on my own in a living hell to the point where I attempted to take my own life.

When I was eventually released, I was placed on a tag for a further six weeks, meaning that I couldn't leave my home at night – a small price to pay for getting out of prison. I was subsequently dismissed from West Yorkshire Police in what I maintain, a decade on, was a grossly unfair process.

Michael's iCan moment
My life was in ruins. I had no money, no job and was a labelled a convicted criminal. My prospects looked bleak and the stress unexpectedly grew. It was at this point in my life that I made the decision to take control and make something of myself.

I immediately signed up for a training course and began my journey to being a qualified sports therapist.

As I was on the course, I began working on the manuscript of my story. I had made some notes while in prison. I also began looking at the prospect of setting up my own business.

In 2000 I graduated from my course and set up a sports injury clinic, which runs to this day with a year-on-year increase in profit and turnover. In 2002 I began a job as a lecturer where

iCan

I qualified as an assessor, verifier and teacher. My manuscript was published in 2008 by HarperCollins and *A Fair Cop* was on the shelves in all the major book shops by November. By this time, I was being asked to events, talks and signings, and the book was selling really well with excellent reviews.

In January 2009 I began my new role as a restorative justice co-ordinator for the local authority where I draw on my police and prison experience to help tackle crime by a process of assessed mediation. I am also writing my second book.

What I love about Michaels's story was his ability to bounce back. During the year of the incident for which he was convicted I was myself released from the very same prison he found himself in. Knowing what prison life was like it really must have been a living hell for him. That year, like him, I thought my own life was in ruins and I also considered taking my life. It just goes to show that no matter how bad things become we all have the ability to bounce back. Life may never be the same again for us, but there is a life waiting to be had.

www.afaircop.co.uk

A Fair Cop
Michael Bunting
The Friday Project, 2009

DON'T ASK, DOESN'T GET

He was by far the scruffiest person in the Costa café at St Pancras station. I was killing time on my way to speak in Chatham, sharing a table with a stranger as the place was crammed full. As I sat eating my chilli panini I noticed this man, about the same age as me, who really looked out of place. He had a suit jacket on like me, but his jeans and Caterpillar boots with no laces didn't seem quite right with me. They didn't with him either as he was hobbling about.

He looked around for a few seconds and then homed in on someone at each table. "Could you spare a few pence towards a cup of tea?" he asked, again and again. It was obvious this chap had fallen on hard times. I couldn't believe how everyone gave their excuses. I wondered how I would have felt if that were me.

iCan

I waited for him to ask me – I would have gladly bought him a cuppa. But he kept looking straight past me. Was I really that unapproachable? I was disappointed that he didn't ask me. I love finding out about people and helping them if *iCan*.

I was beginning to get really disheartened for the man, then, as I got up to leave, a middle-aged lady stood up and offered him what looked like 70 pence. "At last," I thought. This was just great to see. As I walked past him I gave him a smile and whispered "follow me" – which he did. I wondered if he thought I was about to arrest him.

I gave him a comforting smile as we stopped at the other side of the concourse. I discovered he was called Alfred and he had been in the UK for two weeks. He came from Nigeria and was such a softly spoken young man. I asked him why he hadn't asked me and he told me that he thought he already had. I asked him what he wanted the money for and he said it was for a bed for the night, which was going to cost £18. I asked him how many people he had to speak to each day to get his money. "Hundreds," he said. This guy was an inspiration to me – as anyone who has ever achieved any level of success in the world will confirm, nothing in life was ever handed on a plate. Incidentally, I did give him some cash as my instinct told me it really was for a bed for the night.

I originally posted this story to the followers of my newsletter and I got this interesting response from Simon.

"I was on a night out with friends and this homeless guy was sat at his pitch near the NatWest cash machine asking all the passers-by for some change, everyone ignoring him or giving him abuse.

As I approached with my wife he asked me for some change so I asked him 'if I gave you some money what would you do with it?'

I was expecting a reply of 'buy some food', or 'get a bed for the night.' No! He replied 'once I have enough money I will buy alcohol.' His honesty shocked me.

I went to the nearest bar, bought a couple of bottles and took them outside. I sat next to this homeless guy and we started talking. He told me his name was Chris and he had a wife and family but couldn't cope and turned to alcohol. Chris and I sat talking for over an hour before I left him with a few quid.
The following week I was out again and there was Chris in his usual spot. He said 'Hey Simon, got a minute?' so I went to speak to him. I was shocked that he remembered who I was, did I make that much of a difference to his life? I like to think so. I was expecting some patter of 'can you lend me some money' or the like, but no – he had some cash and wanted to buy me a drink!

I declined as I was in a rush but I promised him I'd come back later, which I did and we sat, talked, and I took him some food and a beer. Every time I was out in Liverpool I made sure I saw Chris until one day he was no longer there, I don't know whatever happened to him and I have never found out. I hope he sorted his life out and went back to his family.

But Chris inspired me. I started volunteering for a homeless charity in Manchester, which I did for 3 years, working with the homeless, rent boys, prostitutes, drug addicts and those who just need a free meal."

iCan

Nothing in life worth having will be handed on a plate

(Apart from dried mango, my son Ellis might add).

Like Alfred, anyone in sales knows that you have to work through the rejections. JK Rowling couldn't get a publisher for over a year. It took me months to get an agent interested in what was to be my No 1 Bestselling book. I did think about giving up, but I dug deep and kept going.

What is it that you want to achieve? Are you prepared to work through all the noes, the rejections and the setbacks to get it?

Think of an occasion where you gave up. What did it absolutely stop you from achieving? Could you have gone just a little further? Write it down here:

....

....

....

....

....

Go for No
Richard Fenton & Andrea Waltz
Courage Crafters, 2010

PERSISTENCE PAYS OFF

Sitting on the train on my way back from Blackpool where I was speaking, I picked up an email to my iPhone. The message was from a media student at the University of Leeds who was doing a project about Peter Sutcliffe and wanted to meet me.

As you can imagine, I get requests like these all the time. This particular person has emailed a couple of times and I was impressed by their 'never give up' attitude. I told the student that I was simply too busy and that I have a rule that I don't usually do this kind of interview for students... unless they were prepared to meet me off the train in around an hour's time. I didn't expect that they would be able to get organised in such a short space of time. They had to hire a camera from the University and get to the station to meet me. But no, they texted me to say that the camera was booked out and that they were on their way to the station to meet me. I was blown away by their passion and resourcefulness.

Nothing in life worth having will be handed to you on a plate. (Except a good curry, maybe).

One of the differences between achieving something and not, is having the determination, to give it one last push. *Even if others would throw the towel in and give up.* I learned that

iCan

when I was released from prison and was about to have my home repossessed. I had been given six weeks to get a job, and it looked as if no-one would give me one until I went for my last interview, two days before my home was to be taken. Miraculously, I was offered a job and my turnaround finally began. It was as if someone upstairs was testing me, and tested I was, as I almost took my life a week before I got the job. Of course I didn't succeed, and as you can imagine, two books, 400,000 copies sold, 1000 presentations to more than 125,000 people and most importantly a loving wife and three fantastic children later, I'm over the moon.

Talking of presentations: recently I achieved *another* of my goals by not giving up. You read earlier that in 2006 I spent some time with the coach Jane Kenyon. In the list of 34 things I wanted to achieve, one was to speak internationally. Back then I had only spoken from the stage around a dozen times and speaking outside the UK seemed a very long way off, if at all. As I had a metaphorical magic wand I wrote it down and crossed my fingers.

A few years later I was the closing speaker at The Advantage Travel Conference, which took place in Lucerne in Switzerland. Most of the delegates travelled the world as part of the work they did in the industry, so probably didn't appreciate how big a trip this was for me. It had taken me a few years to achieve the international engagement, but I knew it would happen somehow. Embarrassingly, I had invited someone who represented the speaker agency, who eventually sent me out to Switzerland, to come and see me speak back in 2006 whilst I delivered what was a practice speech for the Professional Speaking Association. (They allowed newer members to have their talked critiqued by established speakers.) I was terrible, but I didn't let that extremely poor performance stop me returning to the agency some time later and finally becoming one of their motivational speakers. *Never Give Up* in action once more. Knowing what I know now about the importance of having goals and having crossed off 20 things from my list of 34, *there isn't a thing on that list that I can't have if I really want it.*

Keep a journal

On my way back to the airport I met a very interesting chap on the train who had attended the conference. During our conversation we began talking about goals and goal setting. He showed me a journal in which he had pictures of all the things that he wanted to achieve in the future. We were both of the opinion that there is nothing that either of us can't have, so long as we decide what it is that we want and focus on it and keep going until we obtain it.

Authors note: When the author suggests never giving up, it does not apply to something that we have been trying to do for many years with no success. If whatever you are doing simply isn't working then you may need to look at your approach. Don't give up on the overall goal, but you may need to change direction slightly in order to achieve it.

READ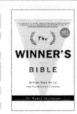

The Winner's Bible: rewire your brain for permanent change
Kerry Spackman
Winners Institute, 2009

iCan

PICK YOURSELF UP

*"Nothing's impossible I have found
For when my chin is on the ground
I pick myself up
Dust myself off
Start all over again"*

— Dorothy Fields

My daughter Skye and I had been visiting this family for weeks; we often took them some food, knowing that food, for them, was scarce. It was obvious that they were not in receipt of benefits. Their home wasn't furnished very well and was surrounded by litter. You can imagine our despair as we arrived close to their home on Wednesday to discover that it was completely gone. There had been heavy rainfall the previous evening and the moorhens' nest had been washed clean away. Skye was visibly upset and asked "Daddy, what going to do?" (she was two at the time). I assured her that they would be fine. We set off around the small lake as I knew there was another nest at the other side. I found myself wondering just what the moorhens *were* going to do. We finished off-loading the half loaf of bread to a collection of birds and we made our way home. I decided to make a detour avoiding the site of the nest on our return journey and we went about our business for the day.

Two days passed before we returned to the lake close to our home. I felt a little sadness, more for Skye who uttered "nest wash away, Daddy," as we approached the site of the nest. I knew we couldn't avoid the area forever so decided to pass anyway. I did a double take as I spotted what Skye did a few seconds after me; there was another nest, which had been built within 48 hours to replace the one that had been washed away so unexpectedly.

"Nest come back. Nest come back," shouted Skye as she dived for the bread, which lay in the basket underneath the pram. I couldn't believe how the two parents had obviously worked tirelessly and probably through the night to provide shelter for the two chicks. I was amazed and blown away by their efforts.

Learn from your setbacks

Observing what those guys did with a handful of twigs, branches, leaves and ice pop wrappers, brought home to me that the ability to deal with life's setbacks is within each and every member of the living world. The young chicks learned a valuable lesson during those 48 hours.

Maybe next time life deals you a blow ask yourself what you can learn from the situation. It's simply a matter of attitude: An *iCan* attitude. Don't leave home without it.

IF YOU'VE DONE YOUR BEST, YOU'RE NOT A LOSER

The life of a motivational speaker allows me insights I would have otherwise missed – although often I wish I *had* missed them. As well as speaking to adult audiences, I often find myself inspiring students in schools around the UK.

iCan

I could not believe what I witnessed recently as I sat waiting to speak to 200 year 9 students. The students were getting a pep talk from a member of the PE staff about the sports day to take place in the coming weeks. I can't remember exactly what he said, but he was urging each of the house teams to pick their best team for each event. He was ranting and raving about how disappointed he would be at anyone finding themselves on the losing teams.

Now, I'm all for encouraging each of us to be the best that we can be … but what if someone is more talented than us in an event? They will achieve better results than we do. Does that mean we should feel bad about not winning? Maybe we will win at something else? He really was giving it to them and I thought about my own children and how I want them to grow at school.

It's OK not to win … Get over it. Most of us will not win at sports day. I don't think I ever did. I was terrible at football and was always on the bench. I don't recall Mr Pointer, the PE instructor, being disappointed at me. It just wasn't my thing. But get me on a stage speaking in front of 200 of my classmates in the school public speaking event … That I did win. It doesn't mean to say the others who took part in the speaking event were losers (although on paper they were).

I received this email from a young person who makes the point perfectly.

…I just wanted to say thank-you for such an inspirational speech at the MIDAS conference in Harrogate on Tuesday. That afternoon I actually took part in the MIDAS speaker competition. I was terrified before, but your speech helped my confidence and although I didn't win, I feel like I accomplished

something by standing up in front of my peers and speaking on the topic of 'Youth Culture'. I even had the confidence to again put myself forward to speak in another activity the next day! Many thanks – Liam Bracey

Give it your best shot

Winning is great and to be encouraged. But if you don't win this time, as long as you gave it your best shot you won't be going far wrong. Never Give Up.

iCan

GET NOTICED

We have two goldfish in our house, called Wilma and John. They can eat for England. One morning, when I was brushing my teeth, I looked in the mirror and I saw Wilma and John trying to get my attention. They were staring at me and moving both their noses (do fish have noses?) frantically in my direction. I ignored them. I went back into our bedroom, then I went back to shave. The same thing happened.

I wasn't having a pair of fishes telling me what to do! As I had more time than I usually do most mornings I decided on a bath rather than a shower. It was superb as I lay there, nice and relaxed, teeth cleaned, face shaved and … hang on. There they were again. Wilma and John were jumping about as if someone had dropped an electric iron into the bowl and they were being electrocuted. I could take no more. I got out of the hot bath and reached over to where we kept the fish food. I took some out and sprinkled it into the bowl. Peace at last.

iCan

Grab their attention

Now I don't know what it is you do or where you are in life. Maybe you work for someone else, have your own business or maybe you are still at school. Whoever you are, you need to get the attention of others (for the right reasons of course). If we are in business we have to stand out from the competition. At work you have to be the one who goes the extra mile so that a promotion arises, you will be more highly thought of.

If you are a young person, take a leaf (or possibly a weed) out of Wilma's and John's book (or bowl): get noticed. And don't give up until you do.

How could you get noticed for the right reasons?

1 ....

2 ....

3 ....

YOU DON'T HAVE TO BELIEVE ME

We recently decided to get a swing for the children for the garden, as they love the ones in the local park. As our garden was big enough, we cleared an area and laid a large square of bark to ensure a soft landing in case of any mishaps. After a few weeks I noticed that we had begun to see a few weeds starting to appear through the bark. I was a little disappointed as I had personally laid the mesh netting that was supposed to stop just such an occurrence. I was picking up the weeds when I came across something that stood out. It looked to be the beginnings of some kind of small bush.

iCan

I pulled up the little twig-like growth and you can imagine my surprise when at the end of the twig was a horse chestnut 'conker' which must have ended up in the bark.

I excitedly called the children over and explained what had happened. They loved it – I suppose it was their first real nature lesson. We planted the horse chestnut in a pot and watered it. It was quite a topic of conversation each week as we watched it grow. I admit that I was probably more excited than they were. One year on this sapling has grown to around a foot in height and we have had to put it in a much larger container. In fact it probably wants transferring into the ground now.

I love this fantastic example of the potential that cannot always be seen at first glance. If the horse chestnut had a personality it wouldn't matter if it believed me, if it knew it or even understood it – the fact remains that it has the potential to grow into a mighty tree that could be around for hundreds of years. And the storms it would undoubtedly endure would make it stronger.

Weather the storm

Whether or not you believe, know or understand it, you have the potential to grow far beyond what you, or those around you, can see now. Things might be tough at times but, like the horse chestnut, you'll weather those storms.

THE iCAN CHRONICLES

iCAN...
CHANGE
MY LIFE

Ian Banyard

I was living what many would call a successful life. I had a large detached home, I was married to a pretty and loving wife with three wonderful children. I owned two cars, we had two incomes, as a family we regularly holidayed abroad. I was successful at school, achieved a degree, I secured a good job with great prospects and a career path. By 1994 I had successfully climbed the corporate ladder. To the outside world I had made it. I was a success. Having grown up in relative poverty, I had created a wealthy and secure home for my children that as a child I could only dream of.

I was a success, so why didn't I feel like one? Despite my success, inside I was frustrated. I felt I was living someone else's life, I was going through the motions of being a loving husband, dutiful son, responsible son-in-law, positive parent, loyal friend, ambitious, committed employee, friendly neighbour and "good" person. For some reason I wasn't connected to my life emotionally. I felt detached, like an

iCan

observer, living my life on automatic pilot. It began to dawn on me that the life I was living was the direct result of the thoughts I had been thinking since my childhood. Wanting to escape my childhood life of poverty, the way I had been thinking had created, a stereotypical ideal of the "perfect life" – the only problem was that this life was everyone else's expectation of me and didn't take into account my desires and my dreams. I had fallen into the habit of trying to please everyone else and forgetting about what I wanted. No wonder I felt so empty.

Ian's iCan moment #1

It was time to change… I realised I had a choice. I could continue living someone else's life or I could start to live my own. Did I want a life by accident or a life by design? I began to study personal development books, listen to tapes and attended seminars. I learned that all successful people visualised their goals and aspirations and listed them down and somehow got what they wanted.

I visualised myself self-employed running my own personal development business, I visualised earning twice as much money doing half as much work, owning a red sports car and working on TV. I visualised my family, happy and healthy, standing outside a big dream house, waving to me. I envisaged swapping my stressful life in the office with a bottomless in-tray and rush hour journeys to and from, for open roads and a workspace surrounded by lakes, mountains, forests and beautiful peaceful landscapes. I wrote these goals down in a book and then over the next 10 years as a direct result of all this positive thinking, *iCan* attitude and wish list, my "merry-go-round" life turned into a rollercoaster ride. At times exhilarating and exciting and at others, it felt like riding Universal Studios' Tower of Terror.

Everything I wrote down and thought about materialised. Some were wonderful but some were not so great. Just a word of advice, when you visualise your happy, healthy family and see them standing, smiling outside your big dream house, make sure you are in the picture too!

Two years ago, I was living in the beautiful English Lake District running a work-life balance company surrounded by lakes, mountains, forests and beautiful landscapes. I could earn twice as much money doing half as much work – just not very often. I was again living the life I had previously visualised. But I felt isolated. I was underachieving and needed a new challenge. I was also feeling frustrated at the lack of British summertime and the abundance of rain and desired warmer climes.

A friend sent me a clip of a motivational speaker with a great story. He'd worked in Saudi Arabia after deciding that he wanted to work abroad and had written a visualisation list. He so inspired me that I decided to focus my attention East. Unknown to me, at the same time in Abu Dhabi, a frustrated training company owner was focusing her attention West.

In January 2006, out of the blue, I received an email from Abu Dhabi asking if I was interested in delivering training to UAE nationals. I Googled Abu Dhabi images and the Sheraton beach club resort caught my eye. It was such a stunning picture of the hotel under a cloudless blue sky with a palm tree-lined, golden sandy beach fronting a beautiful deep blue lagoon, I felt compelled to put it on my screen saver. I responded to the email but heard nothing. I had almost given up on the idea when an email offering a meeting in London arrived. Although it was a long journey, short notice and I still had some doubts, I decided to go. We hit it off straight away and I discovered they used the Sheraton Hotel.

iCan

The Universe delivers... A month later I flew out to Abu Dhabi, I was met at the airport and driven to the Sheraton Hotel. Within 24 hours of arriving I was sitting on the beach under the very same palm trees at the hotel on my screensaver.

Tingles up my spine... There's more, the sea looked gorgeous so I decided to go for a swim. The resort's lagoon was like stepping into a warm bath and the salt content in the water made swimming effortless. I lay on my back and floated on the surface looking up at the blue cloudless sky. Behind me was a diving platform so I swam over and climbed onto it and looked back at the hotel.

Ian's iCan moment #2

At that moment the hair on the back of my neck stood up. I was looking through my own eyes at my screen saver picture. I was actually standing in the exact same place the photographer had stood when the screensaver picture was taken. A picture I found which randomly searching the internet for information about a thought I had six months earlier. I now had my "story".

I absolutely love this chronicle as iCan relate to so much about it: The list of goals, putting them on his pc as a screensaver and allowing the universe to do its work.

www.ianbanyard.com

TAKE CARE – EVERY DAY

I have always hated dentists. So you would have thought that I would do all that I can to ensure that I don't have to visit, apart from of course a check-up. If only life was that easy. When I was younger, I didn't always look after myself as I should. One of the things I was too lazy to do was to brush my teeth regularly. Not too often, but every once in a while, I would skip what I knew I should be doing. Surely it won't make much of a difference. After all they looked OK. And they looked OK when I was 16 until I lay almost horizontally with a large dentist looking down my nose as he probed my mouth with whatever dentists use to carry out a deep root filling.

Earlier that day and completely out of the blue I had found myself in excruciating pain and in desperate need of a dentist. After a check-up it was decided that he would take what was left of the root out and deep root fill it. I was terrified and couldn't wait for my ordeal to be over and before long it was. I vowed never to end up going through that again and I never did. Of course that wasn't the last of it because 25 years later and while I was looking after our third child this neglect of my teeth would come back to haunt me.

I had a glove puppet on my left hand and Isla, aged one, was in my right hand. I'm not sure what my puppetry skills were like, but Isla seemed to be enjoying what I was doing. After the show was over, I went to take the puppet off my left hand with my teeth. All of a sudden, a small gust of air entered my mouth that I wasn't expecting. Two-thirds of my tooth had had broken off. It was the very same tooth that had been deep-root-filled all those years earlier. Aagh! This was late at night and I was speaking in the morning. Luckily, I went to the local chemist who sold me some form of clinical cement that would hold the piece of tooth in place until I could get to a dentist. I was able to give the presentation but we had to abandon the workshop that followed.

Care now means no pain later

I never knew that one day I would lose that tooth. When I was younger and a little lazy, I turned a blind eye to what I knew I should have been doing. On the outside I looked no different to those who were brushing their teeth regularly – but there was a difference. When you add up all those times where I chose not to brush, the outcome eventually meant I lost my tooth. I had to have a crown fitted and although it looked fine it didn't need to be that way.

The young person who plays truant once in a while looks no different to the one who has 100% attendance; the one who eats junk food initially looks no different to the healthy eater. But over time when you compound that junk food they grow to be three sizes bigger and they live six years less. Those who don't put everything into what they do look no different to those who do, but guess what: over time the outcomes will be completely different. It's the compound effect I mentioned earlier in action again.

iCan

THE iCAN CHRONICLES

iCAN... DO ANYTHING AND THAT'S THE WONDERFUL THING

Tim Downes

"Take your glasses off, I might fancy you!"

I took them off slowly and smiled shyly at the schoolgirl engaging with me.

"Yuk! Put them back on again quick!"

I hated school. At eight they discovered, I was extremely shortsighted in both eyes. Poor eyesight had left me behind at learning and making friends. My jam jar bottomed glasses led to name-calling and bullying. Sadly this wasn't just from my fellow pupils. A school teacher I had a crush on painted my face in multiple colours in front of the older boys and girls in her boyfriend's class. They howled with laughter.

For the next few years I matched the poor performance predicted in my school reports and left with zero qualifications. It was made very clear to me that I was going nowhere in life. A career officer took one look at me and decided that I looked like I should go to college to study office work. That was the first step on the path to a too long early career in credit control.

Tim's iCan moment

Then came 1977 and a new attitude for life that set me free. A new positive 'can do' attitude called Punk. It screamed "do anything you wanna do!" Bands like The Clash and songwriters like TV Smith from The Adverts set me free and I developed an "I can do anything" attitude to life.

I recall reading catalystic word balloons in a Legion of Super-heroes' comics. "People get what they want out of life; if you want pain you get pain, if you want happy, you'll get happy." I studied at night school and swapped glasses for contact lenses. My love life and career really began to flourish. At Securicor, where I worked, I developed a flair for leading and mentoring. My team became an award winning team and went on to achieve a series of record breaking performances.

iCan

I moved on to another company, Marshalls, where I grew my team from 6 to 250 and rose up the hierarchy and into the senior management team. Then a series of synchronistic events led to Brian Mayne training my management team in Goal Mapping and Life Mapping.

Tim's iCan moment

I was one step away from my dream of becoming a director when I entered that workshop room. Within those four hotel walls my career changed for good. I can clearly recall sketching the crossroads and footsteps and thinking about my life purpose; I am helping as many people as possible down their chosen path in life.

Within months I became the first full-time executive performance coach in the building and manufacturing industry. I had found my bliss and was totally on purpose.

It was like the first light of a new dawn. Years passed as the rising talent I coached attained true results. It was time to fly solo and I've never looked back.

The I Can attitude conquered my fear of heights and I was soon walking on fire. A coachee asked me what goals I had not achieved. It was time to dare to dream. A few months later I was live on stage with my all time favourite punk band and singer-songwriter singing the magic words...

"We can do anything and that's the wonderful thing".

www.risingtalent.co.uk

ANSWER THE DOOR

By the time I was five, we'd had more than 100 visits from the social services who believed that my sisters and I were at risk of coming to some harm due to my parents' lack of parenting skills. I didn't realise this at the time, but when I recently contacted the social services, it all made sense. The huge file they had kept on us made interesting – but grim – reading. It only reinforced how difficult things had been for Mum back then.

Yes, I may have been at risk as a child, and there are still many children considered at risk in the UK and around the world. But in my experience, many adults are also at risk:

- of underachieving
- of leading an unfulfilled life
- of becoming far less than they have the potential to become

iCan

You've probably come across the kind of person I am describing:

- stuck in a job for 15 years that they do not have the courage to walk away from
- the hair-dresser who can never contemplate working for herself
- the teenager who can go to college but thinks university is beyond them
- the neighbour who always wanted to write their own book but never got around to it

You may be one of those people reading this right now. You may know deep down that you are at risk yourself. That's OK – everyone is at risk. But we don't have anyone knocking on the door checking up on us. Except in rare cases, there will be no big file kept on us by the local authorities. We don't have neighbours spying on us like they were for Mum and Dad.

Think of me as your social worker

What you do have is me knocking on your metaphorical door right now. I give you permission to slam that door in my metaphorical face. You don't need me to have a face-to-face chat with you. In fact, you don't need to have a face-to-face with anyone right now.

Or do you?

What would you really like to achieve?

1 ....

2 ....

3 ....

What might get in the way?

1 ....

2 ....

3 ....

How will you overcome those obstacles?

1 ....

2 ....

3 ....

Stop faffing about and get out there and create the kind of life that is there waiting for you. Yes, the likes of you. It won't be easy but why not you?

Faff: The False Art of Feeling Fulfilled
Mike Pagan
Sunmakers, 2009

iCan

ABOUT THE AUTHOR

Richard McCann is also available as a keynote speaker, workshop facilitator or MC.

He regularly delivers the *iCan Speak Bootcamp* for anyone wishing to improve their communication skills and is available for one-to-one coaching.

He delivers the *iCan Do* personal development day and is co-founder of Teenspeak.

For more details or to book Richard please visit his website. **www.RichardMcCann.co.uk**

Follow him on Twitter @iCanInspire

Also available

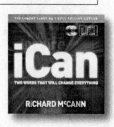

iCan: Two words that can change everything. *Audio Version*

Richard McCann DVD: Speaking Live

Just a Boy

The Boy Grows Up

SPECIAL READER OFFER

Download the audio version of this book for half price:

~~£14.99~~ £7.49

To take advantage of this offer, visit:
www.richardmccann.co.uk/icanoffer

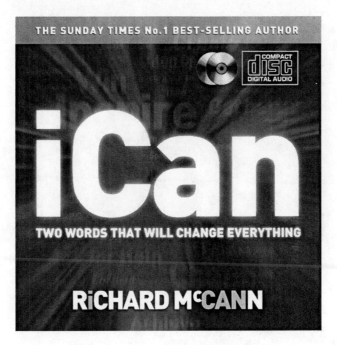

iCan

Notes

CPSIA information can be obtained at www.ICGtesting.com
Printed in the USA
LVOW08s2218170813

348397LV00003B/363/P